Select Effective Visuals

The Business Professional's Guide to Selecting & Creating Effective Presentation Visuals

Dave Paradi

Other books by Dave Paradi:

Present It So They Get It
The Visual Slide Revolution
102 Tips to Communicate More Effectively Using PowerPoint
Guide to PowerPoint (editions for PowerPoint 2003, 2007 and 2010)

Published in Canada and the United States
by Communications Skills Press.

Library and Archives Canada Cataloguing in Publication

Paradi, Dave, 1966-, author
    Select effective visuals : the business professional's guide to selecting &
creating effective presentation visuals / Dave Paradi.

Includes index.
ISBN 978-0-9881549-1-9 (paperback)

    1. Business presentations--Graphic methods. 2. Visual communication.
I. Title.

HF5718.22.P37 2015   658.4'52   C2015-902963-5

Printed in Canada and the United States of America

www.SelectEffectiveVisuals.com

Cover by Rebecca Renner of Creative Minds Inc.

PowerPoint® is a registered trademark of Microsoft Corporation.

Table of Contents

Select Effective Visuals

The Business Professional's Guide to
Selecting & Creating Effective Presentation Visuals

Acknowledgements

Some may wonder why I continue to write books, this being my eighth. It is because of my desire to share what I have learned with others in a way that will help them to create more effective presentations.

One of the people who pushed me to do the thinking that led to this book is speaking coach Tanja Parsley. I lost count of how many times she asked me how I came up with the ideas for the slide makeovers in my workshops. I realized that I did not have a clear enough process or explanation, so I went back and examined exactly how I look at presentation visuals for business professionals. The end result became this book.

I continue to be inspired and grateful for all of the organizations who strive to communicate more clearly and effectively with presentations. They commit the time and effort during my workshops to learn and, afterwards, to apply their learning. When I hear stories of how executives no longer have to ask questions on what is being presented and when senior leaders don't have to spend hours re-doing slides before presenting them to the executives, I know that I am making a difference.

I also want to thank the late Warren Evans, a professional speaker and guide to many in this business. He never stopped encouraging all of us to do better, be more successful, and be better people. I, and many others, will always be indebted to him.

Finally, I would never be able to do what I do if it were not for the support of my family. My wife Sheila edits all my writing and makes it better. It is thanks to her that my books are well organized and clearer. She is also the one who keeps the family strong. Our children, Andrew & Laura, are supportive through crazy schedules and travel. They know how special they are and how this business is our business, not my business.

Introduction

Why did I feel the need to write this book? Because so many business professionals have asked me how I create the slide makeovers that I use in the customized workshops they attend. I take slides that the participants are already using and I show them how effective those slides could be. Naturally, they ask how I do it because they want a repeatable process they can follow.

I am not a designer. I have no graphics background and no design training. I have an undergraduate degree in Chemical Engineering and I have an MBA. So how did I figure out how to select and create effective presentation visuals? Frankly I had to think about the answer for quite a while. Years in fact.

In 2013 I once again started documenting and reviewing how I determine which visual would work in a certain situation. I've done this before, and shared some of my past approaches in my previous books. This time I was determined to find a step-by-step approach that any business professional could use. One that would work for almost any message a business professional would communicate.

In the fall of 2013 I started incorporating my new approach into my workshops. I needed to see how typical corporate presenters would react. Could they follow the approach? Would they find it easy to use? Almost immediately the feedback was very positive. A typical business professional with no design or graphics background could use the model that I had developed.

After teaching this approach for over a year, I decided it had proven its worth in the marketplace and it was time to share it in a book so others could also benefit. The process of writing this book has further refined and focused the approach. I have started using this refined approach in my work and it is effective.

I call my approach the HVF Approach, which stands for Headline, Visual, and Focus. The next chapter gives an overview of the approach.

The main focus of this book is the Visual step in the approach, which is the selection and creation of visuals for slides. Why? Because corporate presenters told me they need the most help with this area. The default approach of using overloaded bullet slides, entire spreadsheets copied from Excel, confusing default graphs, and the occasional poorly formatted diagram is not good enough. Audiences expect more from presenters today.

This book will help business professionals of all levels. If you are in an analyst or specialist role, you will be able to create slides that your executives can use in front of senior management. If you are in a management or executive role, you will have ideas on how to quickly improve the slides your staff creates for you. And when you want to spend less time revising their slides, get them a copy of this book and call me to deliver a customized workshop for the team.

There are almost 200 example visuals in this book and when looking at them you will notice that they are not high end design. There is no shading, gradients, and other techniques designers use. In fact, most of the examples use the default colors for the default PowerPoint template. Why? Because most corporate presenters don't want to become designers and they are restricted by the corporate PowerPoint template as to which colors and styles they can use. I want you to see examples that you will be able to create using the tools you already have and a few extra skills I share.

You will also notice that some of the terms or acronyms on the example visuals aren't easy to understand or don't make sense. That is because many of the examples are taken from the work I have done for my clients. I have tried to keep the slides substantially the same so you can see what that visual looks like in a real presentation. I changed some of the names, terms, or acronyms to hide the identity of the source.

Whenever you see a person's name in an example visual, it has been created from a random name generator and is not the name of the person at my client organization.

The focus of this book is not to list every visual that has ever been created. There are plenty of websites that list a lot more visuals than I have included here. This book will help business professionals select and create the visuals that are most likely to be effective in communicating key messages to business audiences.

In fact, there is a section close to the end of the book that lists a number of visuals that people may have expected me to include, but I left out on purpose. These visuals are excluded because either they do not effectively convey a concise message, or they are mostly used in academic or scientific situations, not business situations. Instead of using these visuals, use the alternative visuals I suggest that work better for business presentations.

There are a number of examples and links to resources that I am not able to include in this book, but I want you to have access to them. So check the last section of the book for the website and password where you can see more examples of great visuals, access written and video tutorials on creating visuals in Excel and PowerPoint, and get any updates to the book after it is published.

I am convinced more than ever before that business professionals can create effective presentation visuals using the HVF Approach in this book. You do not need to have any design or graphics background. You just need the desire to learn and the commitment to apply this approach to your presentations. If you invest the time in improving your presentations, your audience will notice, you will have a greater impact, and your career will advance more quickly.

Overview of the HVF Approach

The three step HFV Approach I use to create presentation slides is:

1. Headline: write a headline that summarizes the key message
2. Visual: select and create an effective visual
3. Focus: use techniques to focus the audience during delivery

The first step, writing a headline that summarizes the message you want the audience to understand from your slide, is very important. If you skip this step, it will be very hard to select an effective visual because you won't know what the visual is supposed to communicate. The best way to get clear on your message is to write it as a summary sentence, which is the headline. The next chapter contains more tips on writing effective headlines.

The second step is to select a visual that illustrates the message you want to communicate. I have created a six category model that will allow any business professional to select and create a visual that will work well for the message. The different visuals are organized within groups and sub-groups in each category. The overall structure is outlined in a subsequent chapter and many examples of the different visuals are provided in the chapters on each category.

The final step is to use techniques that will focus the audience when you deliver the slide. The three techniques I will discuss in a later chapter are: adding callouts, building slide elements, and breaking down complex topics.

By following these three steps, any business professional can create effective presentation slides.

Step 1: Write a Headline summarizing your message

The first step in creating an effective presentation slide is to be clear on the message you want that slide to communicate. What do you want the audience to remember from that slide?

Many business presentations report results, whether they are financial, operating, or market results. Even sales presentations report the results of analysis on the best solution for the problem. You will likely have a number of different results to communicate in your presentation.

It is important to consider what type of results you are presenting if you want decision makers to understand your message and take action. What executives need are actionable insights, but often they only get performance or measurement results. Let's examine each of these three types of results and how they impact the headline you write for each slide.

The most basic results are measurements. It could be measurements of financial, operational, or market activities such as sales, market share, revenues, inventory, expenses, or many other aspects of organizations that are constantly measured. Measurement answers the question, "What did we do?"

The volume of measurement results has exploded in the last decade as it has become easier to measure every activity and organizations falsely believe that more measuring will lead to better decisions. Measurement results are simply numbers. Often they are presented as a data dump from the measurement system or database. On their own, they don't give executives any context to make a decision.

The next level of results are performance results. This gives a measurement result context by comparing it to some standard in order to draw a basic conclusion. The standard could be a previous time period in order to see growth or decline since that time period, it could be a budget or plan figure to see whether the results are above or below what was expected, or it could be an industry benchmark to determine whether the results are in line with others in the industry. Performance results answer the question, "How did we do?"

Performance results are now much easier to generate than in the past due to the power of spreadsheets. Organizations create huge spreadsheets that crunch numbers every imaginable way. The spreadsheets generate plenty of performance results, but when that spreadsheet is presented to executives, it is confusing more than enlightening. The overwhelming amount of data leaves many scratching their heads.

What many executives and decision makers need is the highest level of results, actionable insights. This requires a broader perspective and focuses on longer term goals and objectives. Actionable insights answer the question, "What do we do next?" This requires a consideration of past performance, a projection of future performance, and a determination of whether that will meet the long-term goals of the organization.

Actionable insights are not easy. They can't be generated simply in a spreadsheet. They take thought, consideration, and a deeper examination of the results within the context of the goals the organization is trying to achieve. Creating these insights is a valued skill and one that presenters can use to generate opportunities for advancement in organizations.

Let's look at an example of the difference between these three types of results. A measurement result would be that last month our market share in the East region was 32.5%. The headline for the slide would be "East region market share at 32.5%". On its own, this doesn't mean much. So we compare the market share to last year at this time, and we find that our market share in the East region grew 0.4% in the past year. This looks like a good news story. Let's write a headline saying, "East region market share up 0.4% to 32.5%". Not so fast. Let's look at the bigger picture. The company has been investing significantly in the last nine months in the East region to try to increase market share to

40%. An increase of only 0.4% shows that the efforts are not working the way they are supposed to. The actionable insights are that we should do an honest assessment of the efforts to increase market share and if it still doesn't work in the next two months, the investment should be stopped and we accept that we will only be a mid-tier player in that region. The executives need a slide with a headline of, "Investment in East region market not paying off; time to reconsider future in region".

So why aren't most results in presentations actionable insights? Why do most presenters stop at performance results? One reason is because it isn't easy to create actionable insights. It is much easier to just copy the spreadsheet onto the slide, put a generic title on the slide like "Market Share", and hope the executives figure it out. After all, isn't that why they get paid the big bucks? No. They get paid the big bucks to make the tough decisions of what to do next. They rely on their analytical staff, who are close to the action, to give them the actionable insights from the results.

So how can you go from presenting performance results to presenting actionable insights? The most important change is a change in perspective. To create actionable insights, you have to have a broader perspective and one that is focused on meeting the goals of the organization. Looking at performance compared to last year or even the last three years is not enough. Remember that actionable insights answer the "What do we do next?" question. For that, you need a forward looking perspective.

What specific goal is this area or initiative helping to reach? If you don't know, ask the executive who requested the presentation. Then search out the rest of the story. Look at this result in relation to other results that are helping to reach this goal. Project what will happen in this area given these results and what you know about the trends in the area. Come up with a few possible insights and test each against the data. Check your assumptions and determine what risks exist if an assumption is not correct.

Don't think you need the one correct answer, because there likely isn't one perfect answer. It is OK to give the executives two or three slides with a well thought out insight on each. They can see the different options and choose. Be prepared to answer questions on each insight. Base your answer on your analysis.

This all sounds good you say, but I am just reporting on a project to create a new inventory system for our warehouses. This is the fourth monthly report the steering committee is hearing. What possible actionable insights could I have? Plenty. Let me share some examples. Your analysis of the work versus the schedule should give you insights around the staffing levels, skill levels of staff working on the project, and productivity of in-house and external resources. Your budget analysis should give insights on cash flow timing and how close the original ROI will be. Your analysis of the quality of the system should give you insight into whether the cost savings that were used to justify the system will be met and whether the staff will use the system effectively.

You should be able to recommend actions such as staying the course, making adjustments to scope or resourcing, or even scrapping the effort now instead of investing additional money into a project that has little chance of meeting the goals it was set out to meet. With these clear recommendations as headlines, the steering committee will be clear on what your analysis says. These are decisions you will be asking the steering committee to make based on the actionable insights you present. That is far better than just presenting variance to project plan in schedule and budget, which is what the typical steering committee project update would be.

When you present actionable insights instead of performance or measurement results, others will notice. Executives will see the value of the work you do, and give you advancement opportunities. Invest the time to create actionable insights instead of just reporting measurement or performance results. The investment will pay off.

Once you have determined the actionable insight, what do you do next? Write that insight as a headline, a summary sentence that captures the insight clearly for your audience.

The best example I have found to follow when writing a clear headline is to state it like they do in newspapers. Every newspaper article, whether in print or online, has a headline. It summarizes the key point of the article so the reader can decide whether they want to read the full article.

I would suggest online news sites rely even more on their headlines than print newspapers do. The headline is all the person viewing the home page sees and the headline has to compel the visitor to take the action of clicking on the text to read the full story. In fact, you will see some online news sites change their story headlines during the day to get more people interested in clicking to read the full story.

A headline should be a summary sentence that could stand on its own, even if the visual was not there. You can test how clear your headlines are by flipping through your slides with everything covered up except the headline. Display your slide in Slide Show mode and hold a piece of paper to cover up everything below the headline. Would the audience be able to know the key messages you wanted them to leave with? That is a stiff test, but one that raises the bar and forces us to write headlines that are good summaries of the points we are making.

Not only are headlines good for the audience, but they are also a great aid to the presenter. You have likely seen a presenter display a slide and then look at it with a puzzled expression on their face. They are trying to figure out what the slide means. After an uncomfortable pause, they decide to skip the slide and move on. When every slide has a headline, the presenter just glances at the headline, knows what they need to discuss on this slide, and can confidently deliver the message for that slide. When they have finished that point, they move on to the next slide. There is no fear of forgetting what you wanted to say on a slide.

In a consulting assignment for the CEO of an investment management firm, I emphasized how critical it was that they be clear on the headline for each slide. The presentation helped them retain over $800 million in assets and the CEO told me afterwards that writing clear headlines was the most important advice I had given them. It helped her be clear on her key points and helped her deliver the presentation with confidence.

When I consult with executives on important presentations, it is not unusual that the slide they show me is so confusing I have no idea what message they are trying to communicate. I ask them what the message of the slide is supposed to be. Often they are not clear themselves. They include the slide because it has always been used in the past. Writing headlines forces us to be clear about our messages, which makes our presentation so much more effective. Writing effective headlines is often the one takeaway from my workshops that gets the most positive comments on the evaluations.

If you are struggling when writing a headline because you don't know how to include two key points in one headline, you have run into a common challenge. How do you fit two key messages into a single headline? You don't. If you have two messages, create two slides. Each slide should have its own message and headline. It makes it much easier for the audience and for you as the presenter.

Yes, you will have more slides. But the effectiveness of a presentation is not measured by how many slides you have, it is measured by how clear the message is and whether the audience takes action. It is actually faster for an audience to go through 20 slides that each have one clear message than it is to go through 5 overloaded slides where they have to spend time figuring out what the real messages might be. This is even more obvious when the presentation is emailed. Someone can quickly flip through the deck and know exactly what the key points are because each slide has a well written headline.

It is so important to be clear on the message from the start because the next step in creating an effective presentation slide is to select the appropriate visual. Without a clear message, you won't know how to select the correct category of message and, from there, the group, sub-group, and the specific visual. Get clear on your message first by writing a headline for your slide.

Step 2: Select and create an effective Visual

The selection of a visual for your slide begins with the message that you captured in the headline you wrote in Step 1. Without a clear message, this step will be very difficult, if not impossible.

After analyzing tens of thousands of slides, I have concluded that there are six categories of messages that a typical business presenter will communicate:

1. Comparing numbers/value/size
2. Relationship of sequence
3. Relationship over time
4. Relationship between entities
5. A person, place, or object
6. Example or demonstration

The first step in selecting a visual is to determine which of these six categories your message fits into. Look at the headline you wrote and look for words or phrases that indicate the type of message you are communicating.

In business presentations, the largest category is the first one, comparing numbers/value/size. As discussed in the previous chapter, so much of a business presentation is typically focused on presenting results, which usually involves numbers. But that is not the only category of visual you will be using, so take a moment to find the best category.

In each of the categories, I have organized the visuals into groups and sub-groups to make it easier to select the best visual. The next two pages show you how the 66 different visuals are organized in the six categories.

Categorized list of all visuals

Category 1: Comparing numbers/value/size

Group	Sub-group	Visual	Page
Comparing values to a standard	The standard is a single value	Dashed line on line graph	26
		Dashed line on column graph	29
		Dashed line on bar chart	32
	The standard is a scale	Stoplight dashboard	34
		Horizontal scale	37
		Vertical scale	40
		Ranking	42
Comparing values to each other	Single data series	Column graph	46
		Bar chart	50
		Proportional objects	53
		Grouped item comparison	57
		Table of insights	60
	Ranges of values	Bar chart of ranges	63
		Column graph of ranges	65
	Multiple data series	Multiple width overlapping column graph	67
		Diverging stacked bar chart	71
		Multiple series proportional objects	76
		Multiple series table of insights	78
		Small multiples	81
Showing components of a total or whole	One component compared to the total	Pie chart	86
		Donut graph	89
		Speedometer graph	91
		Single 100% stacked bar chart	93
		Single 100% stacked column graph	95
		Simple treemap	96
		Multiple 100% stacked bars	99
		Multiple 100% stacked columns	102
		Multiple 100% diverging stacked bars	103
	Components explain a difference	Waterfall chart	105
		Steps to a total graph	109
	One component is broken down into sub-components	Stacked bar breakdown chart	112
		Stacked column breakdown graph	116
Showing a trend	Single data series	Single line graph	119
		Area graph	123
	Multiple data series	Multiple line graph	125
		Dual axis line graph	129

Category 2: Relationship of sequence

Group	Sub-group	Visual	Page
Linear from start to finish	Single path	Chevrons	135
		Shapes and arrows	138
		Shapes on an arrow	141
		Numbered list	144
	Multiple paths	Decision tree	146
		Parallel paths	150
Continuous or loop		Circle and shapes	153
		Shapes and circular arrows	155

Category 3: Relationship over time

Group	Visual	Page
Duration of events is shown	Gantt chart	161
	Calendar with duration shapes	165
Only when event occurs is shown	Simple timeline	169
	Calendar with event indicators	172

Category 4: Relationship between entities

Group	Visual	Page
Hierarchical relationship	Bullet point list	177
	Organizational chart	179
	Breakdown diagram	182
Geographic relationship	Map	184
Comparison	Table	188
Mathematical relationship	Equation diagram	193
	Calculation	197
Group of items	Text points	201
	Text in shapes	203

Category 5: A person, place, or object

Group	Visual	Page
Showing the size of an object	Group of icons	209
Little or no explanation required	Full screen image	213
Explanation required	Image with callouts	218
	Image with captions	221

Category 6: Example or demonstration

Group	Visual	Page
Written format	Highlighted text	225
	Quote	228
	Case study	230
Multimedia format	Audio clip	234
	Video clip	236

The following six chapters cover each of the categories. Within each chapter you will see an introduction to the category, an explanation of the groups and sub-groups in that category, and each of the visuals that fall in that category.

For each visual, I will show examples of that visual, what situations it works well for, and some instructions and tips on creating that visual in Excel or PowerPoint. You may use other software and many of the instructions will apply, but I focus on the most common software that business presenters use. The instructions and tips will help you efficiently create visuals that are easy to understand.

Category 1: Comparing numbers/values/size

The largest category of visuals is the one that deals with showing numbers visually. The default approach in too many presentations is to simply copy the spreadsheet used for the analysis onto the slide and attempt to go through all the numbers with the audience. This usually does not work.

I have organized the visuals in this category into the following groups and sub-groups:

- Comparing values to a standard
    - The standard is a single value
    - The standard is a scale
- Comparing values to each other
    - Single data series
    - Ranges of values
    - Multiple data series
- Showing components of a total or whole
    - One component compared to the total
    - Components explain a difference
    - One component is broken down into sub-components
- Showing a trend
    - Single data series
    - Multiple data series

One of the methods of grouping is by the number of data series being compared. A single data series has one value for each measurement category. An example would be the sales in a single region over the last four quarters. The measurement categories are the four quarters, and there is only one value, the sales for the region, in each category. Multiple data series have more than one value for each measurement category. An example would be the sales in three regions over the last four quarters. For each measurement category, there would be three values, one for each of the regions.

On the following pages in this very long chapter, you will see all of the visuals in this category organized by the groups and sub-groups listed above.

Each group will have an introductory page that explains more about the sub-groups for that group and has a list of all of the visuals in that group. At the top of the page for each visual you will see how it is categorized under the category, group, and sub-group. If you need to see a list of all of the visuals in this category, refer to page 20 in the introduction to Step 2.

Category 1: Comparing numbers/values/size

Group 1: Comparing values to a standard

The first group in this category is messages that compare values to a standard to determine whether the performance is below, meeting, or exceeding the standard. Messages in this group often contain words or phrases such as: above, below, goal, target, standard, or average. There are two sub-groups.

Sub-group 1: The standard is a single value

This sub-group contains visuals that allow the measured values to be compared to a standard that is only one value.

Sub-group 2: The standard is a scale

This sub-group contains visuals that compare the measured values to a pre-determined scale.

Here is a list of the visuals in this group:

Sub-group	Visual
The standard is a single value	Dashed line on line graph
	Dashed line on column graph
	Dashed line on bar chart
The standard is a scale	Stoplight dashboard
	Horizontal scale
	Vertical scale
	Ranking

Sub-group 1: The standard is a single value

Dashed line on line graph

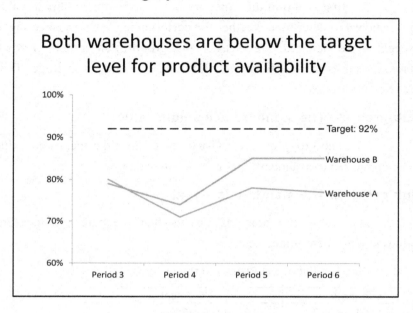

By showing the standard as a dashed line, it is easy for the audience to compare the trend for each data series to the standard. Line graphs work well if you are showing the trend over time.

Examples of usage:

- comparing the trend in product availability to a goal
- comparing the trend in account balance to a minimum required in order to avoid fees
- comparing the trend in speed of answering customer service calls to a promised level of service

How to create and use this visual

An easy way to add the line for the standard value is to add another data series to the graph. This is the series for the standard you are comparing to and all points have the same value. Format this line to be a dashed line. It will always be in the correct place on the graph, regardless of whether the graph is sized later or not. This method has been used in the graph above.

Make sure you use labels in the graph to indicate which line is the standard and what the other lines represent. You can add text boxes for these labels if you want. You can also use the Data Label feature of Excel or PowerPoint to add a label containing just the Series name to one of the data points for each line. This method ensures that the labels are tied to the data and will move when the data values change.

Additional examples

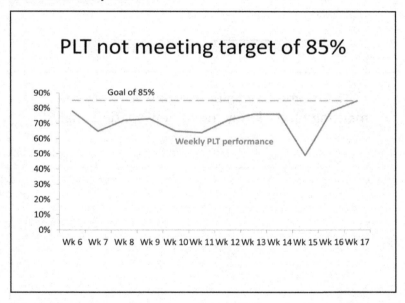

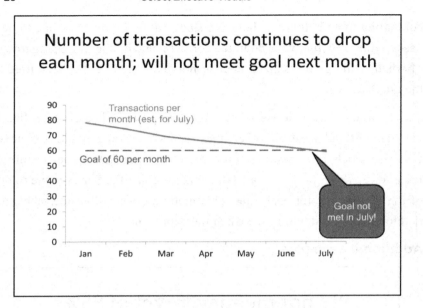

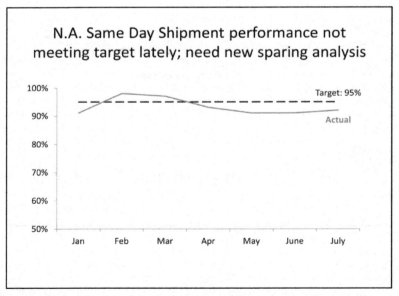

This example adds data labels for the series name on the last data point of each line. Unlike text box labels, these labels will stay in position if the graph is resized or moved.

Categorization: Comparing numbers > Comparing to a standard > Single value

Dashed line on column graph

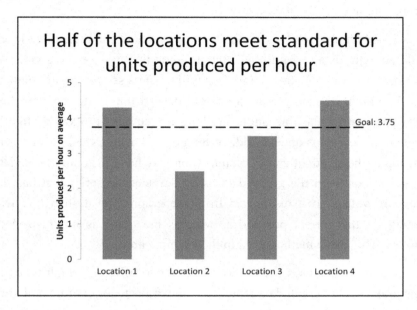

By adding a dashed line to indicate the standard that the values are measured against, the audience can quickly see if the performance is above or below the standard. Column graphs work well if you are showing measured values that are not time based (line graphs, like the previous visual, work better for time based information).

Examples of usage:

- comparing spending in one region to an average of other similar regions
- comparing on-time delivery performance to a standard
- comparing survey form completion performance to a goal in each of six clinics
- comparing performance in different regions against the national goal

How to create and use this visual

There are two methods for adding the dashed line to a column graph and positioning it correctly.

Method 1 involves manually drawing the line at the correct level. Add an extra data series to the column graph that has the same value as the standard for each data point. This will create a second set of columns on the graph. Manually draw a straight dashed line (hold the Shift key down to restrict the line angle) as long as required to extend slightly beyond the columns on each side of the graph. Position the line so it is at the top of the standard value columns (you may have to zoom in the view to get it exact). In the graph data table, deselect the series that has the standard values so it disappears from the graph. The dashed line will remain in the correct position as long as the graph is not resized or moved. This is the method used in the example above.

Method 2 uses the ability to have two different graph types in one graph. In the graph data table, add an extra category before and after the data for the columns. This will create a blank column to the left and right of the existing columns. Add another data series and set the value for all of the categories, including the blank categories, to the same standard value. This creates a set of columns at the standard value. Switch this data series to a line graph chart type and set the line to be a dashed line. This creates a dashed line in the correct position that extends past the set of columns in each direction. This ensures that the dashed line will always be in the correct position even if the graph is moved or resized. This method doesn't always look good if there is a vertical axis, so it is usually used when you replace the vertical axis with value data labels at the top of each column (as shown in the example on the top of page 31).

Additional examples

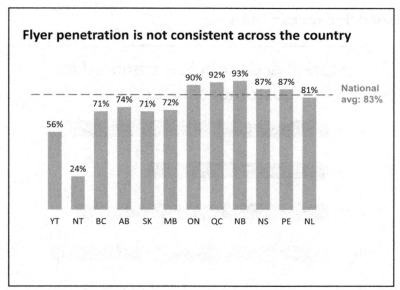

This example uses the second method for adding the dashed line to the column graph.

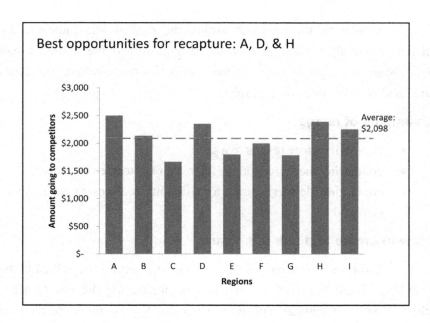

Categorization: Comparing numbers > Comparing to a standard > Single value

Dashed line on bar chart

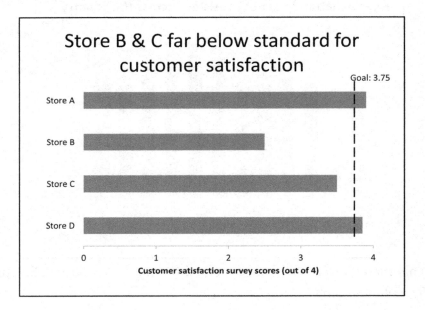

Similar to the previous visual, the dashed line indicates the standard that the values are measured against and the audience can quickly see if the performance is above or below the standard. Bar charts are an alternative to column graphs.

Examples of usage:

- comparing store results to a goal
- comparing measured values to an average to see variance
- comparing delivery times to different locations to an industry standard

How to create and use this visual

Unlike adding a dashed line to a column chart as described in the previous visual, there is only one method for adding the line to a bar chart. You must manually position a vertical line on the slide because there is no built-in type of graph that will draw a vertical line. Use the instructions for Method 1 in the previous section on page 30 to draw and position a vertical line accurately after the bar graph is created.

Additional examples

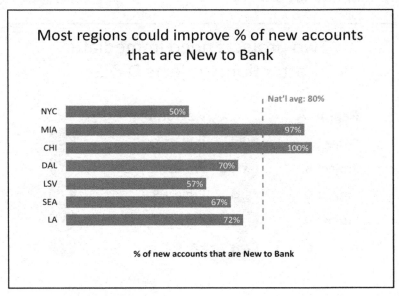

Sub-group 2: The standard is a scale

Stoplight dashboard

This visual is popular with executives because it tells them the areas that need attention at a quick glance. A red, yellow, or green circle is used to indicate poor, acceptable, or good performance on different metrics.

Examples of usage:

- to give a quick snapshot of areas needing attention in a financial report
- give current and future status on project health criteria
- give an indication of performance against goals in different areas

How to create and use this visual

In addition to color coding, the letters inside the circle help people with red-green color deficiency to easily determine what the color is. It is important that everyone is clear on what calculations are done to determine the color for each metric. Without agreement on what constitutes a green, yellow, or red performance level, arguments can ensue regarding the measurement and interpretation. This is especially important where the management style is to criticize any areas with a red level of performance. When creating this type of visual, use the Align and Distribute features of PowerPoint to make the circles line up with each other and be evenly distributed in the columns.

Additional examples

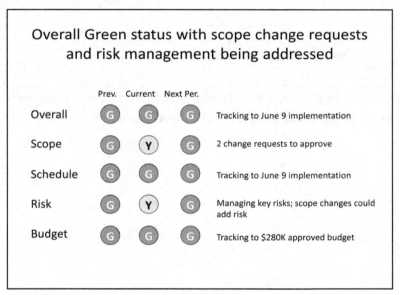

(examples continue on next page)

City 11 Week 26 YTD
RST Scorecard Results YoY

Achieved	G ↑1.5	Responsiveness to Customer Defects	G ↑17.2%
% Orders Scanned	G ↑0.2%		
% of Inspection Lots Performed	R ↑6.4%	Reviewer Resolution of Receiving Errors	G ↑9.7%
% of Revenue Verified	R ↑3.5%	Reviewer Resolution of Verification Errors	G ↑2.9%
Resolution of Receiving Errors via PDT	G ↑0.6%	Timely Completion of Machineable Results	G ↑0.8%
Responsiveness to Product Flow	G ↓0.5%		
% of Confirmed Verification Defects	G ↑10.0%		

This stoplight dashboard adds additional information and focuses attention using rectangles around certain items.

Categorization: Comparing numbers > Comparing to a standard > Scale

Horizontal scale

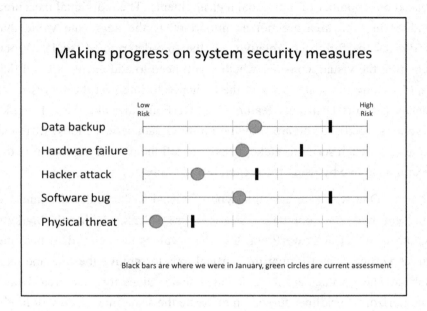

This visual shows where the value for each measured area lies on a scale. You can show one data series, or multiple data series, as the example above shows. The black bars represent the value of each metric in January, and the green circle indicates the value today.

Examples of usage:

- to show how a piece of equipment measures on the criteria used to make a purchasing decision
- to show current position on a scale compared to a previous position
- to show amount of movement from a starting point to the current state

How to create and use this visual

As in the stoplight dashboard, it is important that everyone understands the different values along the scale for each metric and the formula used to calculate the value of each metric. This type of visual works well when you are calculating an aggregate score for a metric based on a number of individual measurements. The individual measured values in each area are not as important as the aggregate value that indicates performance relative to the pre-determined scale. When creating the visual, consider whether you need to add evenly spaced tick marks along the scale to allow the audience to interpret the scores more easily (use the Distribute feature of PowerPoint to make the tick marks evenly spaced). If you are showing multiple data series, choose different shapes for each series to make it easier to tell them apart (as shown in the example above by using the rectangle and circle).

One way to create this type of visual if the scales are numeric and you have only one data series is to use a Scatter with only Markers graph in Excel or PowerPoint. Use the y-values to evenly distribute the areas vertically and format the vertical axis to remove the line and axis labels. The x-values are the calculated scale values for each area. Leave the horizontal gridlines turned on to create the scale lines. You will likely have to increase the default marker size so that they are easily seen and you can add data labels if you want each individual value to be shown. The first example below is created using this method. This method will not work with multiple data series because Excel or PowerPoint will not allow you to have more than one set of x-values on this type of graph.

Another option for creating this type of visual is to use a table to create the scale. The first column on the left will be wide and contain the description of each area. The rest of the columns, which will be narrow, create space for the scale. Add a character in the appropriate cell in the table representing where the value is located along the scale. You may want to only have bottom borders between the rows in order to separate the different areas. Having a vertical bar in the first and last column of the scale cells gives a visual reminder of each end of the scale. The second example below uses this method.

Additional examples

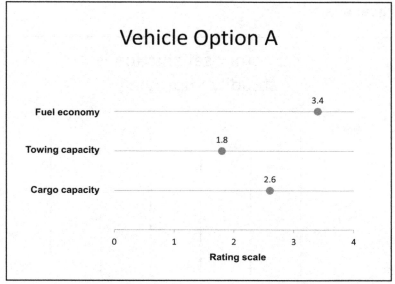

This example uses the Scatter with only Markers graph.

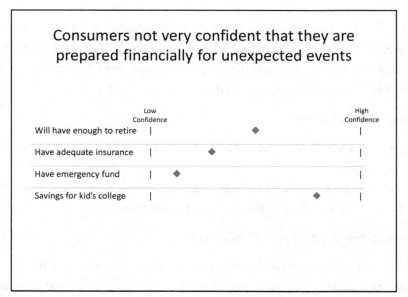

This example uses a table to create the scale.

Vertical scale

This visual is similar to the horizontal scale except that the x and y axis are switched. The areas being measured are along the bottom, and the scale being used to measure each area goes from the bottom to the top. This visual can measure one data series or multiple data series.

Examples of usage:

- to show how a measure of service or satisfaction changes over time
- to show how two vehicles measure on the criteria being used to evaluate which vehicle should be purchased

How to create and use this visual

Creating a vertical scale is very similar to creating a horizontal scale, the x and y axes have just been switched. You can use the method of drawing the lines and shapes manually, using the Align and Distribute features of PowerPoint to evenly distribute the lines. As in the other scale visuals, it is important to understand the calculation of the value along the scale.

This visual can also be created using the Scatter Plot with Markers graph in Excel or PowerPoint. Follow the general guidelines described on page 38 for the horizontal scale visual. Because this type of graph allows multiple y-values for each x-value, you can use it to plot multiple data series on the same graph, as illustrated in the first example below.

The table method of creating the horizontal scale visual can also be adapted to create this visual. The table will have many rows and few columns for this visual.

Additional examples

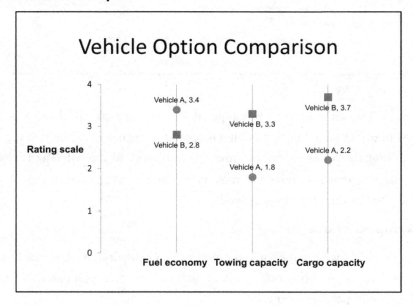

Categorization: Comparing numbers > Comparing to a standard > Scale

Ranking

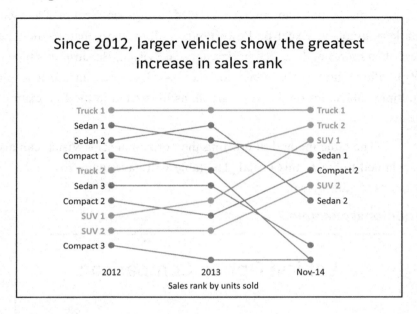

The scale used in this type of visual is a ranking of the values instead of the actual values being compared to each other. The ranking is from highest to lowest shown from top to bottom of the list. The typical message is to show how the rank has changed over time, although it could be between locations as well.

Examples of usage:

- to show how the top ten products in a category change over time
- to show how one product gained in rank compared to the competition over time
- to show how the top products in one territory differ from another territory

How to create and use this visual

This visual is a line graph with markers. When using the rank (ie. 1 to 5) as the y-axis value, you will have to reverse the y-axis so the highest ranking item (rank 1) is at the top of the graph. You can customize the shape and size of the markers, and use colors to emphasize the one or few items that illustrate your point.

Additional examples

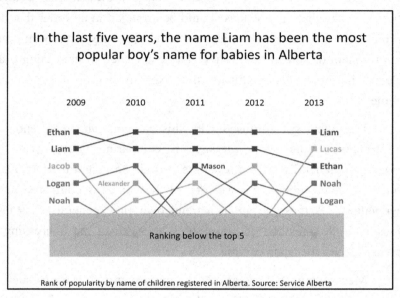

In the last five years, the name Liam has been the most popular boy's name for babies in Alberta

| 2009 | 2010 | 2011 | 2012 | 2013 |

Ethan · Liam
Liam · Lucas
Jacob · Mason · Ethan
Logan · Alexander · Noah
Noah · Logan

Ranking below the top 5

Rank of popularity by name of children registered in Alberta. Source: Service Alberta

Category 1: Comparing numbers/values/size

Group 2: Comparing values to each other

The second group in this category is messages that compare values to each other. The values should be arranged in an order that help communicate the message, not just the order they may have been output from a system or spreadsheet. They can be arranged in increasing order, in decreasing order, geographically from west to east, or in certain cases by time.

Presenters get confused with this category and the trend over time category. When your message is comparing values over time periods, you generally have a few time periods only, and the message is about how much higher or lower one of the values is compared to the other values. A message about a trend over time generally has more values and the message is about how the values are increasing or decreasing over that span of time.

Messages in this group often contain words or phrases such as: best, worst, most, least, highest, lowest, largest, or smallest. When speaking about the comparison, words such as previous year, previous quarter, last year, same quarter last year, projection, budget, or plan may be used. There are three sub-groups.

Sub-group 1: Single data series

This sub-group contains visuals that compare the values in only one data series.

Sub-group 2: Ranges of values

This sub-group contains visuals that compare a range of values instead of individual values.

Sub-group 3: Multiple data series

This sub-group contains visuals that compare the values in two or more data series.

Here is a list of the visuals in this group:

Sub-group	Visual
Single data series	Column graph
	Bar chart
	Proportional objects
	Grouped item comparison
	Table of insights
Ranges of values	Bar chart of ranges
	Column graph of ranges
Multiple data series	Multiple width overlapping column graph
	Diverging stacked bar chart
	Multiple series proportional objects
	Multiple series table of insights
	Small multiples

Sub-group 1: Single data series

Column graph

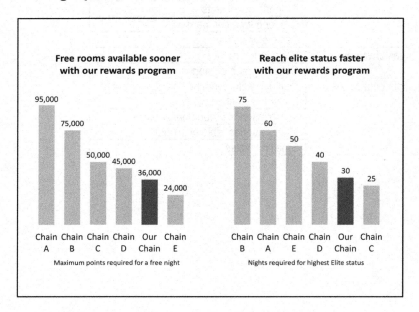

A column graph uses the height of each column to represent the values. The audience can easily see which column(s) are higher than other columns.

Examples of usage:

- comparing results between locations
- comparing success rates in different age ranges
- comparing popularity of different options selected by customers

How to create and use this visual

A column graph is one of the built-in graphs in Excel and PowerPoint. When creating the graph, make sure you arrange the data in an order that fits the message you are communicating. If the headline of the slide does not clearly indicate the measurement, make sure you label the vertical axis so the audience understands the graph.

When using a column graph, do not manipulate the measurement axis to make the difference between the columns look more than it really is. The audience will quickly determine that you are trying to misrepresent the data.

When formatting a column graph (or many of the graphs in this section), there are a number of decisions you should make in order to ensure the graph is clear for the audience:

- Are the values important? If the values are important for the audience to see, consider adding data labels showing the values and removing the vertical axis (as shown in the example above). You don't need both value data labels and the axis since they communicate the same information.

- Should one value be emphasized? If one value is important to understanding the message, make it stand out. Use a muted color for all the other columns, and a bold color for the one column that is most important. The example above uses this approach.

- Does the category axis need lines to define the categories? By default the category axis, the x-axis in a column graph, is formatted with a horizontal line and tick marks to separate the categories. This formatting is often not necessary, as the columns easily stand on their own with just the column labels. If this is the case, remove the line and tick marks to make the graph cleaner.

- Does separating groups of data make the message clearer? If there is a natural grouping of the values within the single data series, consider separating the two groups visually in the graph. You can add a blank category that will create a space in the graph between the two sets of columns, or you can add a vertical dashed line to separate the two groups.

- Will filling the column with an image add to the message? If you are comparing values that represent countries, sometimes filling the column with the flag of that country will add meaning to the graph. Don't overuse this technique, but consider when it could add to the impact of the graph.

Additional examples

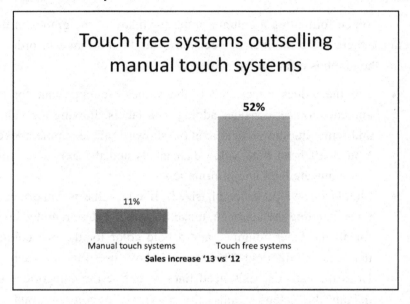

This example did not have one value that needed to be emphasized, so the same color is used for all columns.

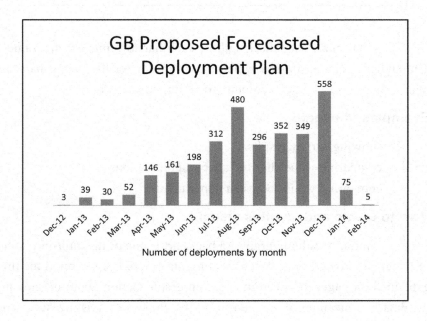

Categorization: Comparing numbers > Comparing values > Single data series

Bar chart

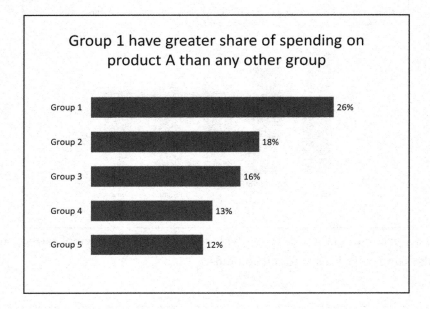

A bar chart uses the length of each bar to represent the values. The audience can easily see which bar(s) are longer than other bars. In many ways, a bar chart is a column graph turned sideways.

Examples of usage:

- showing survey results
- comparing values between geographic regions
- comparing values between departments

How to create and use this visual

Similar to column graphs, a bar chart is one of the built-in graphs in Excel and PowerPoint. When creating the graph, keep in mind the tips explained on pages 46-48 in the column graph section about organizing the data in a meaningful way, ensuring the choices of axis measurement do not distort the data, and formatting the graph so it is clear.

Additional examples

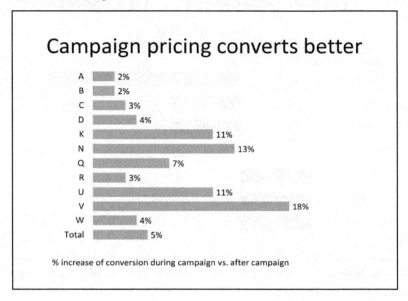

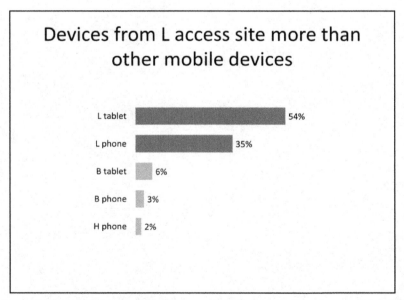

This example shows how the bars you want to emphasize can be filled with a bold color and the other bars filled with a muted color.

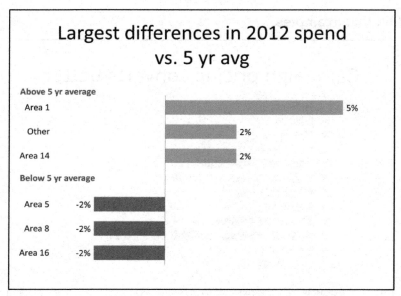

This example shows bars that can represent both positive and negative values on the same graph.

Categorization: Comparing numbers > Comparing values > Single data series

Proportional objects

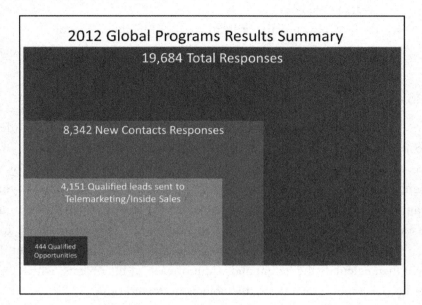

A proportional object collection diagram compares values using shapes that have areas proportional to the values. The shapes can be simple shapes like squares, rectangles, or circles, or they can be more complex shapes and even images. The important aspect of this type of visual is that the area of the shape accurately represents the value.

This type of visual works particularly well when the values you want to compare are different by an order of magnitude or more. With such a great difference between values, a bar or column graph doesn't work because the smaller number almost disappears on the graph due to the graph being limited to measurement in only one dimension. A proportional object collection diagram gives you two dimensions to work with and allows smaller numbers to be more easily compared to larger numbers.

Examples of usage:

- to show how small the leads were from the large number of flyers mailed out
- to show how low the utilization was of the plant capacity
- to show how small the market penetration is of the total prospects in the area

How to create and use this visual

This type of visual is not built into Excel or PowerPoint. In order to make sure the size of each shape is an accurate representation, you must calculate the areas of the shapes, not just scale a single shape by a percentage in one or both directions. To perform these calculations, you can use the Proportional Object Collection Calculator at www.ProportionalObjectCollectionCalculator.com. This tool will ask for the size of the largest object and the values that you want to represent. It will then calculate the height and width of each of the objects, which can be used as inputs when sizing the objects in PowerPoint.

When you are comparing values where each value is a sub-set of the previous larger value (like the example above), overlapping the shapes gives the audience a visual representation of the comparison. This works well for the results at different stages of a sales contact process, the process of selecting the best candidates from a larger pool of candidates based on certain criteria, and any process where the end result is arrived at by eliminating some of the original possibilities using different criteria during the process.

A proportional object collection diagram where the shapes do not overlap is a replacement for a column or bar chart and can give added visual variety to your presentation.

Additional examples

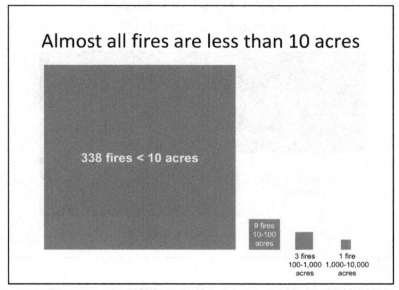

This example shows the shapes beside each other instead of overlapping.

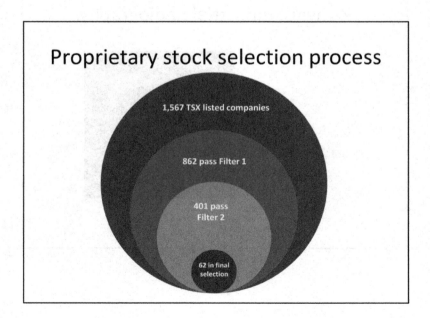

Only 15% of projected market has an RDSP

Projected market: 500,000

75,000 RDSP accounts opened

Radiation dose in 15 seconds from X-ray vs. Industrial Radiography

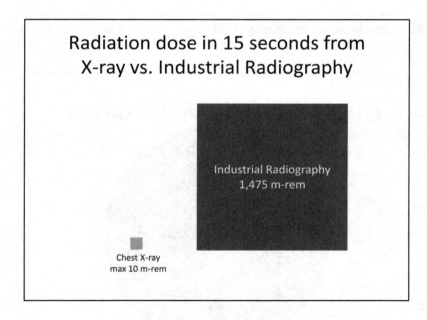

Industrial Radiography
1,475 m-rem

Chest X-ray
max 10 m-rem

Categorization: Comparing numbers > Comparing values > Single data series

Grouped item comparison

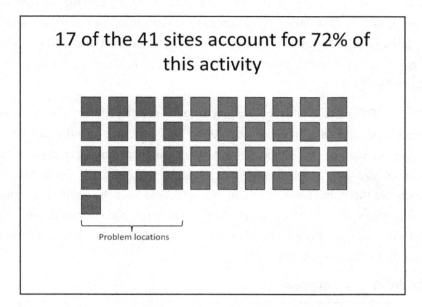

A grouped item comparison visual illustrates the values using a group of items, squares in the example above. The items can represent one unit of the measurement, or multiple units of the measurement, as long as all items represent the same number of units. A portion of the item is used to represent a fraction of the units one full item represents.

Examples of usage:

- you are comparing two or more values and want an alternative to a column graph or bar chart

How to create and use this visual

This type of visual is not built into Excel or PowerPoint. You create the visual by drawing the shapes and positioning them. The items used in this type of diagram can be simple shapes, such as circles or squares, or more complex, like icons of people to represent population statistics.

To make sure each shape is the same size, it is usually best to create one shape first, then copy and paste it to create the other shapes. You can use the Align and Distribute tools to make the shapes line up and be evenly distributed. You can use the Grouping tool to group a row or column of shapes and then copy the group to create the visual quickly. Once you get familiar with these techniques, it is much easier to create this type of visual.

To create a partial shape when each shape represents more than one unit or the value includes a fraction of a unit, it is usually easiest to cover up part of the shape. To do this, create a rectangle that is the correct size and is filled with the Slide Background fill color option. Then use the Align tools to line up the rectangle over the right or left side of the shape. Since the rectangle is in front of the shape, it will cover up the portion you do not want and it looks like the shape was cropped exactly to the desired size.

Additional examples

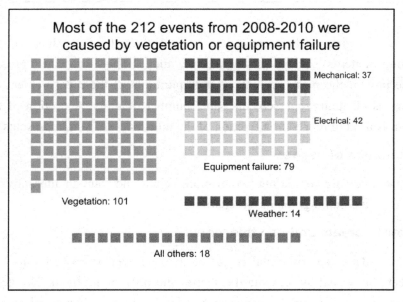

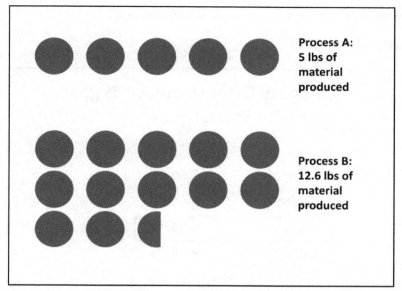

This example uses the technique of covering up part of one of the shapes with a rectangle to represent a fraction of one unit.

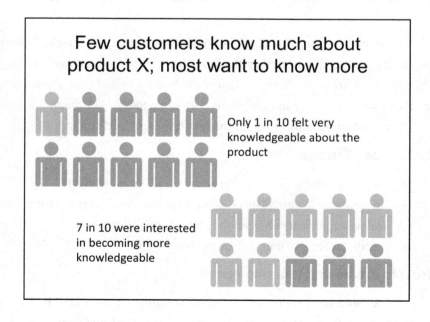

Categorization: Comparing numbers > Comparing values > Single data series

Table of insights

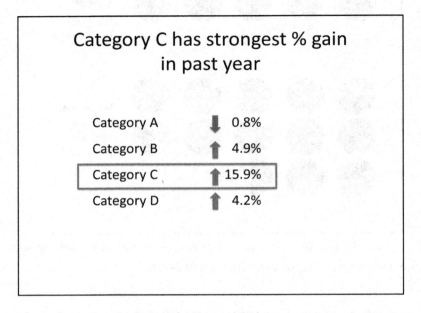

A table of insights shows only the key figures in a table format so the audience can compare the important numbers without wading through an entire spreadsheet. It is usually helpful to add indicators, such as the arrows in the example above, to give the audience an idea of whether the number shown represents good or poor performance.

Examples of usage:

- communicating only the key numbers from an analysis
- to replace a spreadsheet with just the final results from the calculations instead of all the steps in the calculation
- as an executive summary of the results

How to create and use this visual

A table of insights can be created using either a text box or a table in PowerPoint. It can also be created in Excel and copied to the slide.

The advantage of using a text box in PowerPoint is that you can build each row in the table of insights and focus the audience on only the information you have just revealed (building by rows is not available when using the table feature of PowerPoint). When using a text box, use the Tabs to set a consistent position for each column of information. Use the Decimal Tab to make numbers align perfectly without using extra spaces (which never work perfectly anyways).

You can also use the Table feature of PowerPoint to create a table that can easily have a border around one or all cells, as well as ease the alignment of information into columns. When aligning numbers in a column, use the Decimal Tab to make sure each number is aligned properly.

If you create the table in Excel, make sure you understand what will be copied to PowerPoint when you use the different copy and paste methods. Some methods paste the table as an image, which can't be changed in PowerPoint. Some methods also copy the entire Excel workbook, possibly exposing confidential data in other parts of the workbook.

The visual indicators you add can be graphic shapes or special characters. You can use the arrow line or block arrows available as PowerPoint shapes to create indicators (this is the method used in the example above). Remember when animating a text box, you must also animate these separate slide elements in conjunction with the associated text. The alternative is to use special characters. These are treated as text so they are easier to build using animation. They are added by inserting a Symbol in the text (this is the method used in the example below). I have found the Webdings character set contains many useful arrows, thumbs up/down, and other symbols that work well as indicators of the direction of a number.

Use color as well as direction to tell the audience whether a movement is favorable or unfavorable. An up arrow is not always favorable, such as when costs go up. The color helps to interpret the meaning of the direction of the movement.

You can use highlighting or boxes to focus the audience on specific numbers in the table of insights that you want them to pay extra attention to.

Additional examples

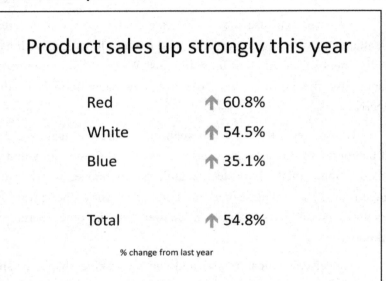

Categorization: Comparing numbers > Comparing values > Ranges of values

Sub-group 2: Ranges of values

Bar chart of ranges

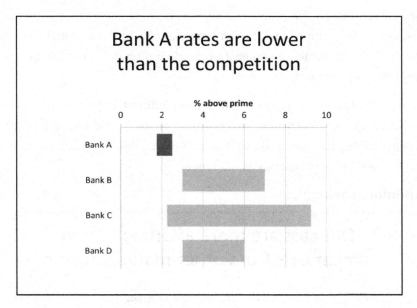

A bar chart that compares ranges of values uses the length of the bar to represent the range and the position of the bar to represent where the range lies on the horizontal axis of all values. The audience can easily see both of these details in the visual.

Examples of usage:

- comparing the range of prices for one category of products to other product categories
- comparing the range of rates charged by one institution to competing institutions

How to create and use this visual

This visual can be created in Excel or PowerPoint using a stacked bar chart. The data contains two segments for each category. The value of the first segment is the minimum value of the range so that the start of the range is positioned correctly along the axis. This segment is set to No Fill and No Line so it is invisible (I refer to this often as the spacer segment). The value of the second segment is set to the range to be represented on the graph. This segment is set to a fill color that is visible on the graph. As with other graphs, you can use a muted color for the data that is not to be emphasized and a bolder color for the data you want the audience to focus on.

In this visual I often find that including the gridlines helps the audience quickly determine the position of the range and the relative lengths of the different ranges. The gridlines can be set to a lighter color so they are not as prominent as the ranges.

Additional examples

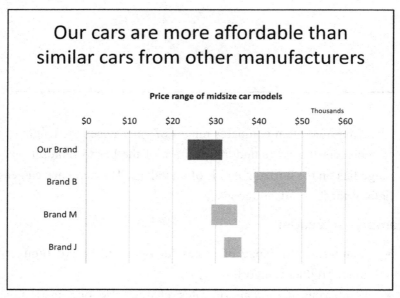

Categorization: Comparing numbers > Comparing values > Ranges of values

Column graph of ranges

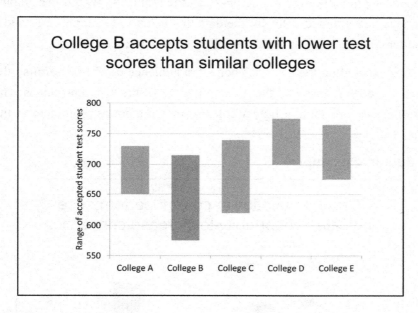

A column graph that compares ranges of values uses the length of the column to represent the range and the position of the column to represent where the range lies on the vertical axis of all values. The audience can easily see both of these details in the visual. This visual is similar to the previous visual and either can be used in most situations.

Examples of usage:

- comparing the range of test scores for admitted students to colleges in the same geographic area
- comparing the range of maximum temperatures that different pieces of equipment can be safely operated in

How to create and use this visual

This visual can be created in Excel or PowerPoint using a stacked column graph. The approach is similar to the stacked bar chart used to create the previous visual on pages 63-64. The data contains two segments for each category. The first segment is an invisible spacer segment so that the start of the range is correct along the axis. The visible second segment represents the range on the graph. As with other graphs, you can use a muted color for the data that is not to be emphasized and a bolder color for the data you want the audience to focus on.

Including the gridlines helps the audience quickly determine the position of the range and the relative lengths of the different ranges. The gridlines can be set to a lighter color so they are not as prominent as the ranges.

Additional examples

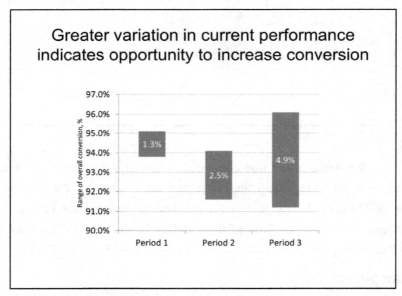

Since the amount of variation is important to the message, this example uses data labels to indicate the range in each column.

Categorization: Comparing numbers > Comparing values > Multiple data series

Sub-group 3: Multiple data series

Multiple width overlapping column graph

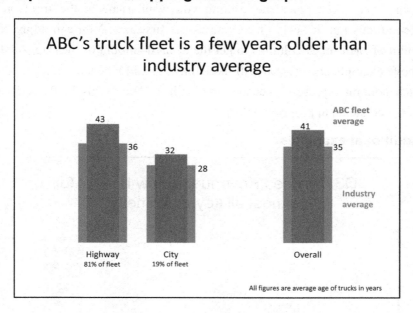

A multiple width overlapping column graph uses the height of each column to represent the values. By placing one set of columns in front of the other set of columns, it is easy for the audience to compare the related columns and see which column is higher. This visual replaces a column graph that has two or more columns beside each other to show the comparison.

Examples of usage:

- when you are comparing current year to past year sales
- comparing your results to the industry average
- comparing current inventory to inventory last quarter

How to create and use this visual

To create a multiple width overlapping column graph, start with two columns in a clustered column graph where the columns are beside each other. Then place the column you want to be in the front on a second axis that is scaled the same as the first axis. You can adjust the width of each set of columns to get the desired amount of overlap. As the above example shows, you will likely have to add labels to indicate what each column represents because the built-in data labels in PowerPoint won't create an appropriate label.

Additional examples

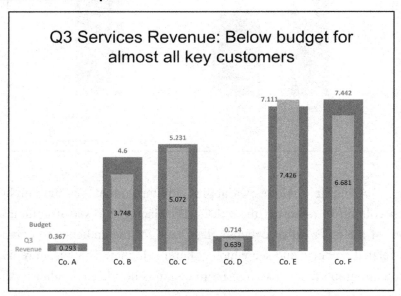

Depending on the spacing in the graph, this example shows how you may have to position some of the data labels inside the columns.

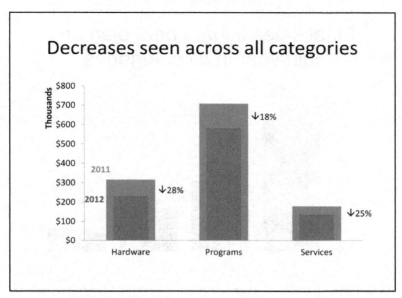

When the % change is more important than the values, you can add text box labels as shown in this example.

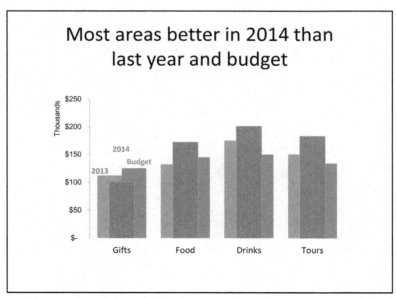

This example shows how you can compare three data series on one graph by moving one column in front of the other two columns.

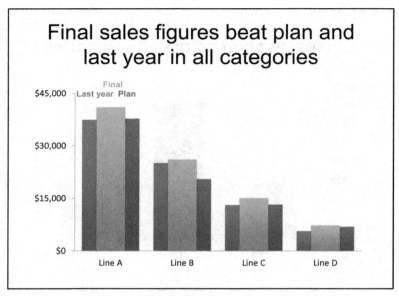

This is another example of showing three data series compared on one graph.

Categorization: Comparing numbers > Comparing values > Multiple data series

Diverging stacked bar chart

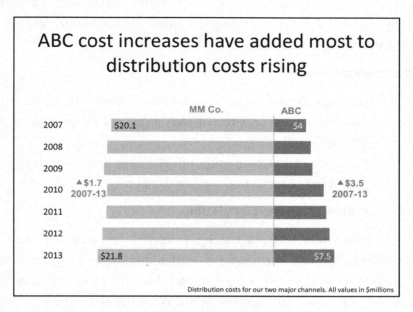

A diverging stacked bar chart is a bar chart that can have one or more segments on each side of a dividing line. The dividing line separates the two (or more) data series. The segments to the left of the dividing line start at the dividing line and grow to the left as the values increase. The segments to the right of the dividing line start at the dividing line and grow to the right as the values increase. All the segments on both sides of the dividing line in one bar represent one category. The above example has only one segment on each side of the dividing line and the two data series are MM Co. and ABC. The categories are the years 2007 to 2013.

The reason that this type of graph works well is that it allows the viewer to compare 1) the sizes of each category by using the total length of the bars, 2) the size of each data series in each category by comparing the length of the segment on each side of the dividing line, and 3) the change in each data series across the categories by looking at the segments on one side of the dividing line. In the above example, it is easy to see that 1) the total spending increased slightly each year, 2) much more is spent with MM Co. than with ABC each year, and 3) the growth in the ABC spending was much greater than the growth in MM Co. spending.

Examples of usage:

- showing how each call center performs compared to the standard
- showing how the opinions of each group are on one side or the other of neutral
- showing how the proportion of sales reps achieving their goal number has changed over the last three years

How to create and use this visual

This visual is created using a stacked bar chart in Excel or PowerPoint. The values are ordered so that the segments appear in the correct sequence from left to right in each bar. The two challenges are: 1) getting the values for each segment correct, because the segments to the left of the dividing line use negative values, and 2) getting the sequence of the values correct, because the sequence is not as it appears from left to right. I have created the Diverging Stacked Bar Chart Calculator at www.DivergingStackedBarChartCalculator.com that will help you do the calculations and create a results table that you can copy into the graph data table in Excel or PowerPoint.

After the graph is calculated, you will likely want to do the following formatting to make it look good:

- For the vertical axis, set the categories to display in reverse order, remove the tick marks, and set the category labels to display at the Low position so they appear to the left of the bars.
- For the horizontal axis, set the minimum and maximum values so that the bars are as long as possible, then turn off the horizontal axis because the negative values are confusing.

- For the built-in data labels to display the negative values as positive values, you will have to use a custom number format (I explain how to use custom number formats in the article at http://paradi.link/Issue331). Alternatively, you can use text box labels.

Additional examples

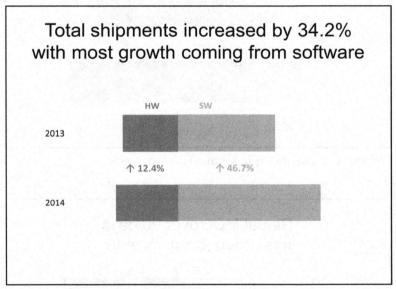

This example uses text box labels.

(examples continue on next page)

This example shows multiple segments on each side.

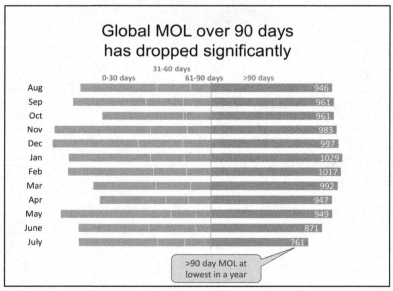

This example uses color to show that the one segment on the right is the most important segment for the message.

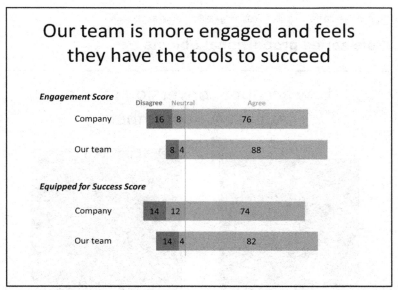

Each bar in this example represents 100% of the answers to a survey. The segment representing positive answers is placed on the right side of the dividing line and segments for the neutral or negative answers to the left of the line. This allows us to easily see on which side the majority of the responses lie.

Categorization: Comparing numbers > Comparing values > Multiple data series

Multiple series proportional objects

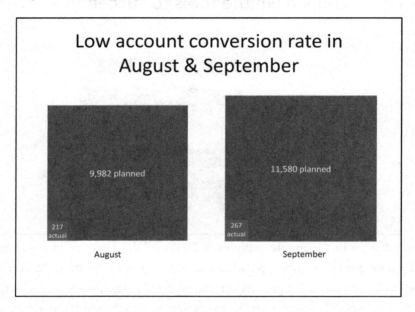

A proportional object collection diagram for multiple data series compares values using shapes that have areas proportional to the values and are arranged so that the data series are easy to distinguish. The shapes are usually simple shapes like squares, rectangles, or circles.

Examples of usage:

- when you want to show achieved contracts vs. proposals sent out in multiple time periods
- when you want to show a comparison of pay scales between full time and part time workers in different positions

How to create and use this visual

This visual is created using the same approach as the proportional objects visual on page 53. When you have multiple data series, you will usually have overlapping shapes because the message is to compare values within each data series or between data series. When creating this visual, make sure that you are consistent in making the shapes proportional with all the related shapes on the slide. If this is not possible, put a dashed line between the groups to visually separate them for the audience.

Additional examples

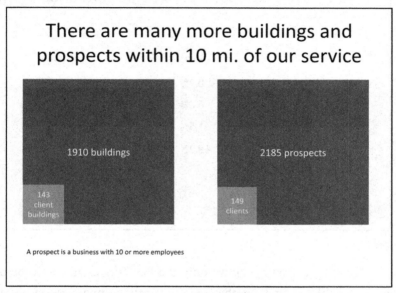

The example above shows two data series where the comparison is within each series, not between series as the first example showed. Here, the shapes do not all have to be proportional to each other because the units in the two data series, building and prospects, are not the same.

Categorization: Comparing numbers > Comparing values > Multiple data series

Multiple series table of insights

> ### Category D far down against plan and last year, other categories mixed performance
>
> | | vs. Plan | vs. Last year |
> |---|---|---|
> | Category A | ↓ 0.2% | ↑ 1.2% |
> | Category B | ↓ 0.6% | ↓ 1.3% |
> | Category C | ↑ 1.5% | ↓ 1.2% |
> | Category D | ↓ 18.2% | ↓ 13.8% |

A table of insights shows only the key figures for multiple data series in a table format so the audience can compare the important numbers without wading through an entire spreadsheet. As with a table of insights for a single data series, it is usually helpful to add indicators, such as the arrows in the example above, to give the audience an idea of whether the number shown represents good or poor performance.

Examples of usage:

- communicating only the key numbers from an analysis
- to replace a spreadsheet with just the final results from the calculations instead of all the steps in the calculation
- as an executive summary of the results

How to create and use this visual

Creating a table of insights for multiple data series is very similar to creating a table of insights for a single data series. Refer to the tips and techniques listed in the section on tables of insights for a single data series on page 60. To line up the arrow character indicators underneath each other in a text box or table, use a tab stop in the ruler (that is how the arrows in the example above are lined up).

Additional examples

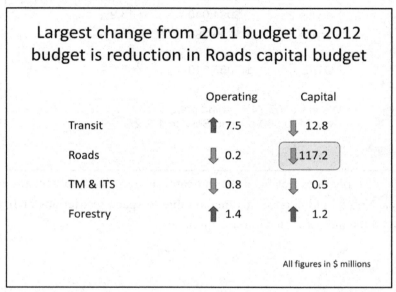

This example shows the use of a highlight and shape to focus the audience on the one number that is most important in the table.

(examples continue on next page)

We are behind plan; need to focus efforts in remainder of FY

	Plan	Current Performance
Service 1	$4,862,320	⬇ 2.3%
Service 2	$994,040	⬇ 13.9%
Service 3	$199,280	⬇ 26.2%
TOTAL	$6,055,640	⬇ 5.0%

We are $303,745 behind plan;
over $120,000 each in Service 1 & 2

This example does not have the indicator arrows lined up beneath each other. You would choose this method due to space restrictions or if you wanted the indicator closer to the numbers.

Categorization: Comparing numbers > Comparing values > Multiple data series

Small multiples

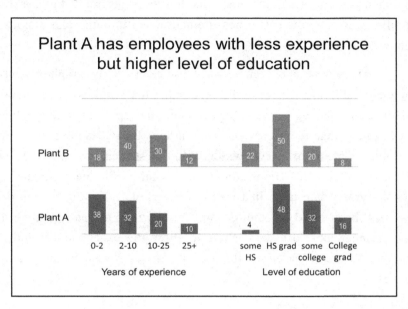

A small multiples visual is really a number of column graphs or bar charts arranged so that you can compare the patterns in multiple data series more easily. It replaces charts that have multiple columns or bars beside each other.

Examples of usage:

- comparing two locations on three different criteria
- comparing two sales teams on sales of the different products offered and the service plans offered
- comparing performance of different age groups on three different criteria

How to create and use this visual

There are two basic approaches to creating a small multiples visual. The first approach is to create separate graphs and arrange them. You can make the graphs the same size using the measurement settings for the graph on the Graph Format ribbon in Excel or PowerPoint. You can arrange the graphs using the Align tools in PowerPoint. With this approach you only need one graph that has the measurement axis as long as all graphs have the same measurement axis minimum and maximum values.

The second approach is to use a stacked column graph or stacked bar chart built into Excel or PowerPoint. This requires some math to calculate the spacing between the segment that represents one graph and the segment that represents the next graph. I have created the Small Multiples Calculator at www.SmallMultiplesCalculator.com that will help you do the calculations and create a results table that you can copy into the graph data table in Excel or PowerPoint. This is the approach that has been used in the examples shown. You can remove the measurement axis, use data labels to show the exact values, and use gridlines to create baselines for each graph (as shown in the example above).

Additional examples

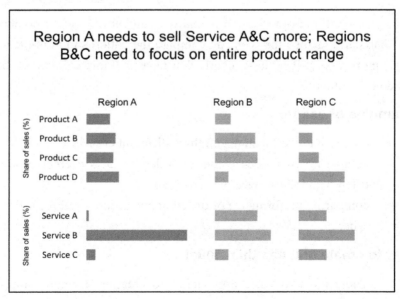

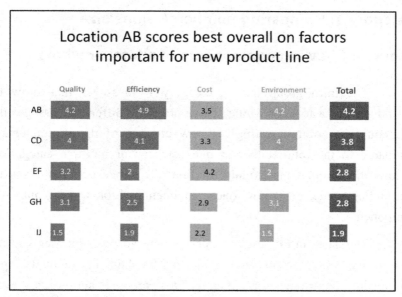

This example shows the use of data labels.

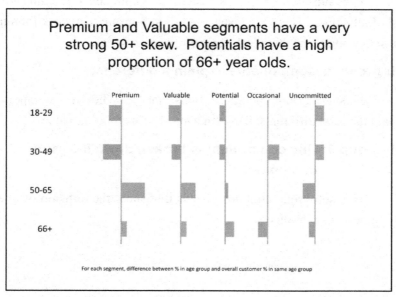

This example shows the use of diverging bar charts as the multiples. The vertical dividing lines for each data series are added by hand in this case.

Category 1: Comparing numbers/values/size

Group 3: Showing components of a total or whole

The third group in this category is messages that show the components of a total or whole. There are three different messages that you could be communicating: 1) how big one of the components is compared to the total (either in one category or multiple categories), 2) how the components explain the total difference between a starting and ending value, or 3) how one component is broken down into sub-components.

Messages in this group often contain words or phrases such as: part of the whole, proportion, majority, breakdown, segments, split, components, contributed, or add up to. There are three sub-groups.

Sub-group 1: One component compared to the total

This sub-group contains visuals that compare one value to the total of all values. There are visuals in this sub-group that work for single data series and some that work for multiple data series.

Sub-group 2: Components explain a difference

This sub-group contains visuals that show how the components explain the total difference between a starting and ending value.

Sub-group 3: One component is broken down into sub-components

This sub-group contains visuals that show the division of one of the components into pieces.

Here is a list of the visuals in this group:

Sub-group	Visual
One component compared to the total	Pie chart
	Donut graph
	Speedometer graph
	Single 100% stacked bar chart
	Single 100% stacked column graph
	Simple treemap
	Multiple 100% stacked bars
	Multiple 100% stacked columns
	Multiple 100% diverging stacked bars
Components explain a difference	Waterfall chart
	Steps to a total graph
One component is broken down into sub-components	Stacked bar breakdown chart
	Stacked column breakdown graph

Categorization: Comparing numbers > Components > One vs. total

Sub-group 1: One component compared to the total

Pie chart

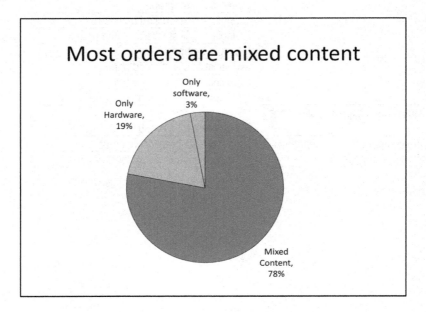

A pie chart divides a circle into two (or more) wedges. The colors you choose focus the audience on one wedge of the whole pie.

Examples of usage:

- when there are two types of events you want to show and a breakdown of proportion of the events in each type
- when you want to show all the proportions, but want two related components to be the focus of the discussion because they are the most important

How to create and use this visual

A pie chart is a standard graph type in Excel or PowerPoint. The mistake that presenters often make is using a pie chart to compare the wedges to each other. Comparing values to each other is a message best communicated using a bar chart (or other visuals) as explained in Group 2 of this Category starting on page 44. A pie chart should only be used when you want to communicate how big one component is of the total.

Sometimes you will only have two wedges, which is easy to create and understand. Sometimes, as shown in the example above, you have more than two wedges, but only one is the focus of the message. And sometimes you have more than a few wedges with two related wedges being the focus. An example of this situation is shown below. In all cases, you should make the wedge(s) of importance a bold color, and the rest of the wedges a muted color. You can add a thin outline around the wedges if you want the audience to see that there are more than two components in the total.

As with other graphs described above, create a clean pie chart by replacing the legend with data labels. The data in the pie chart should be organized so that the wedges of focus start at the twelve noon position of the circle and move clockwise from that spot.

Additional examples

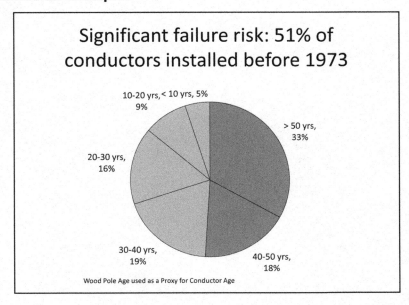

Significant failure risk: 51% of conductors installed before 1973

< 10 yrs, 5%
10-20 yrs, 9%
20-30 yrs, 16%
30-40 yrs, 19%
40-50 yrs, 18%
> 50 yrs, 33%

Wood Pole Age used as a Proxy for Conductor Age

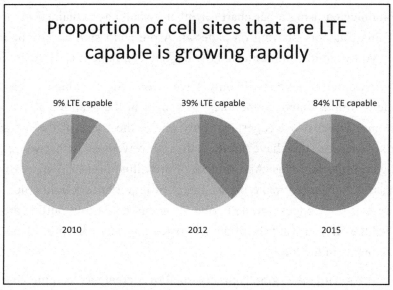

This example shows multiple pie charts where the proportion of the total grows from 2010 to 2015.

Categorization: Comparing numbers > Components > One vs. total

Donut graph

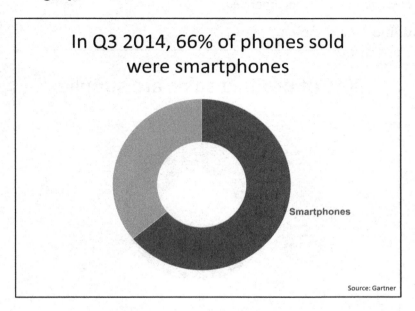

A donut graph is very similar to a pie graph. The size of the donut segment indicates how big that component is of the overall amount.

Examples of usage:

- showing the market share of one product amongst competing products in a country
- showing the proportion of the desired response to a survey question
- showing the proportion of our sales from one product category in the last year

How to create and use this visual

A donut graph is a standard graph type in Excel or PowerPoint. It is very similar to a pie chart and the same formatting suggestions of usage of color to divide segments and indicate the segment of focus should be applied. Similarly, the use of data labels instead of a legend, and starting the segments at the twelve noon position and moving clockwise should be incorporated.

Additional examples

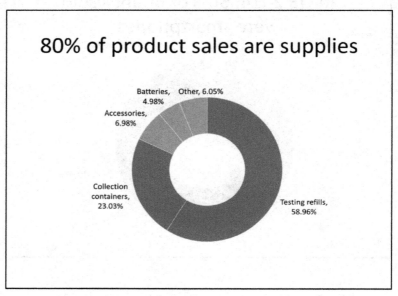

Categorization: Comparing numbers > Components > One vs. total

Speedometer graph

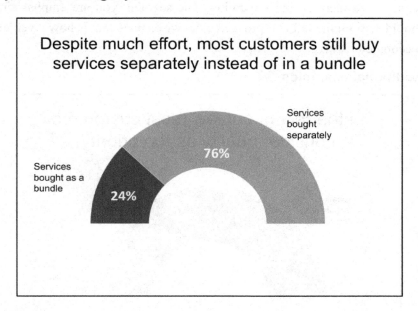

A speedometer graph is half of a donut graph. It only compares two segments and the dividing line between the segments is similar to the needle on a vehicle speedometer.

Examples of usage:

- showing the split between two answers to a survey question
- showing the split between two options a consumer can choose when buying a product
- showing the split between those who accept an offer and those who don't

How to create and use this visual

A speedometer graph is created using the built-in donut graph in PowerPoint or Excel. Half of the graph is set to No Fill and No Line so it is invisible and the entire graph is rotated 90 degrees counter clockwise so the visible segments are as shown above. A muted color is used for the less important segment and a bold color is used for the segment you want the audience to focus on. You can also use an outline around the segments to increase the separation. The segment you are emphasizing should start on the left and proceed clockwise, since that is how a vehicle speedometer works.

Additional examples

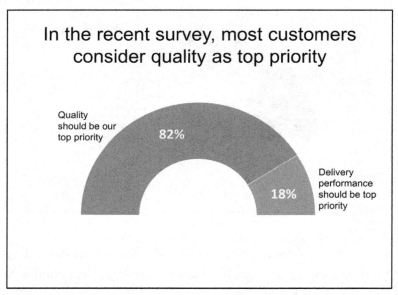

Categorization: Comparing numbers > Components > One vs. total

Single 100% stacked bar chart

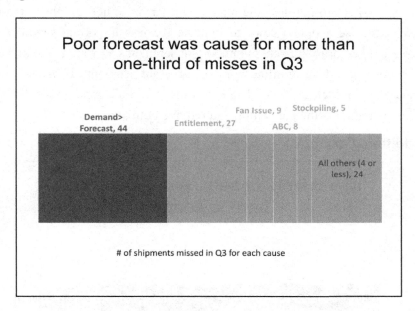

A 100% stacked bar chart divides a single horizontal rectangle into segments that are proportional to the values they represent.

Examples of usage:

- showing the split between positive and negative responses in a poll
- showing the % of total sales in three product categories where we want to focus on one category
- showing the split of all responses to a satisfaction survey for a college course where the focus is on the lowest rating

How to create and use this visual

A 100% stacked bar chart is a built-in chart in Excel and PowerPoint. The advantage of this chart type over a standard stacked bar chart is that this type of chart allows you to enter values without first converting them to percentages. The graph will automatically create the segments as a percentage of the total.

When formatting the chart, similar to other graphs already discussed, use a muted color to indicate the less important segment(s) and a bold color to indicate the important segment you want the audience to focus on. Add an outline color to separate segments if needed. To make the graph cleaner, use data labels instead of a legend, make the bar wide by reducing the gap width, and remove both axes.

Additional examples

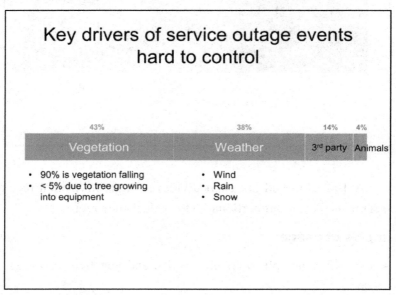

Categorization: Comparing numbers > Components > One vs. total

Single 100% stacked column graph

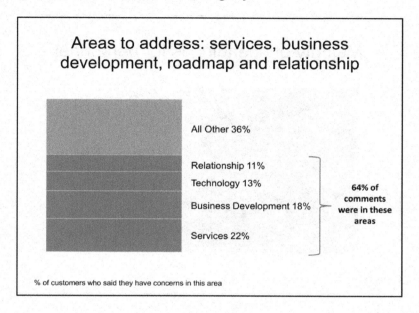

A 100% stacked column graph divides a single vertical rectangle into segments that are proportional to the values they represent.

Examples of usage:

- showing the asset mix in a portfolio where one category is of concern
- showing the split of comments on a survey indicating areas to be prioritized

How to create and use this visual

A 100% stacked column graph is a built-in chart in Excel and PowerPoint. It is created using the same approach described on page 93 for the 100% stacked bar chart.

Categorization: Comparing numbers > Components > One vs. total

Simple treemap

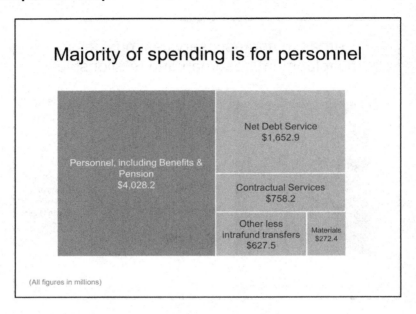

A treemap is a type of visual that allows you to visually compare the size of one value to the rest of the values in a total amount using proportionally shaped rectangles that are arranged into an overall rectangle that represents the whole or total of the different values. It is an alternative to a pie chart. It tends to work best if you have one value that is over 50% of the total of all values.

Examples of usage:

- how the spending in one area is larger than the spending in all other areas combined
- how one company holds more market share than all the other competitors in the industry
- how one department is bigger than all the other departments in terms of headcount

How to create and use this visual

A treemap is not a built-in chart in Excel and PowerPoint. As originally conceived by Ben Shneiderman, a treemap can be much more complex than the examples shown here. In a business setting, a simplified version should be used because the complex version will confuse the audience.

To create the visual, you need to create rectangles that are proportional to the values in the total, and size them so that they all fit together to form a larger rectangle. To attempt this by hand would be time consuming and frustrating.

To make creating a simple treemap easier, I have created a calculator at www.SimpleTreemapCalculator.com that does the calculations for you. To make the calculator work, I had to make some assumptions about how the rectangles would be arranged. In the treemap created by the calculator, the rectangles are always arranged starting with the largest rectangle on the left side of the area for the treemap. The next rectangles then fill in the remaining area from the top to the bottom. The final two rectangles split the last space remaining in the overall area used for the treemap. You can see this pattern in the example above.

The output of the calculator is a list of the exact sizes for each of the rectangles that make up the treemap. Draw the rectangles in PowerPoint and set the height and width of each according to the list of sizes.

I have found that the easiest way to make the rectangles fit together is to turn on the Snap objects to other objects setting in PowerPoint. This makes it easy to drag the rectangles together. I suggest arranging the rectangles with no outline so that they fit together properly. Then you can add an outline to each rectangle to make the individual rectangles easier to see (both the example above and the one below use a white outline around each rectangle).

As with other visuals where you want one value to be the focus of the audience, use a muted color for all the rectangles except the one you want the audience to focus on.

Additional examples

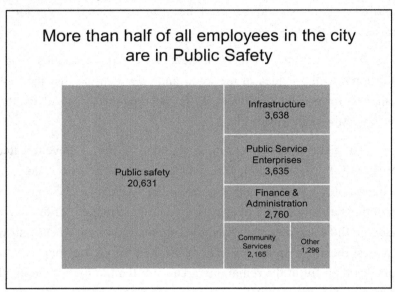

Categorization: Comparing numbers > Components > One vs. total

Multiple 100% stacked bars

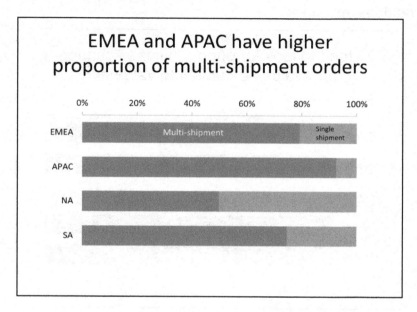

Multiple 100% stacked bars allows you to show how the proportion of one segment changes across regions, time, or another dimension.

Examples of usage:

- showing the split between positive and negative responses across four years of polling
- showing the % of the total sales represented by one product category in different regions
- showing the split of all responses to a satisfaction survey for different college courses

How to create and use this visual

This visual is created by adding data for multiple categories in the built-in 100% stacked bar chart in Excel and PowerPoint. Similar to

the single 100% bar chart, use colors to indicate the important data and
labels instead of legends.

Additional examples

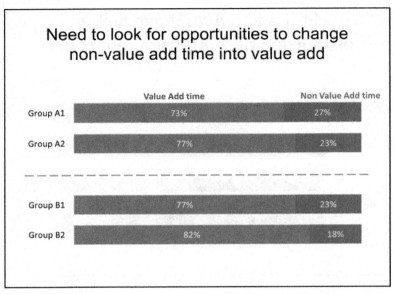

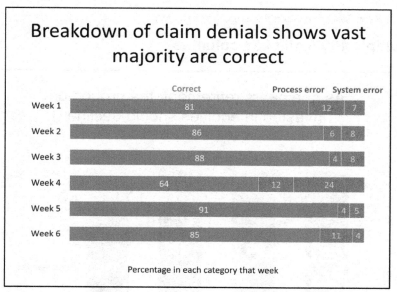

This example (and the one below) show more than two segments in the bars. I would recommend not having more than four segments in the bars for this visual.

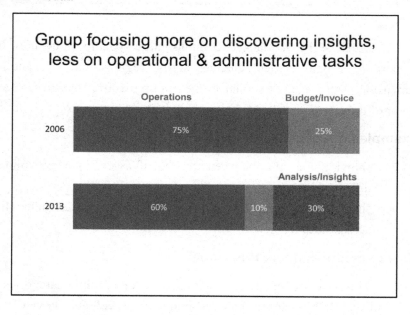

Categorization: Comparing numbers > Components > One vs. total

Multiple 100% stacked columns

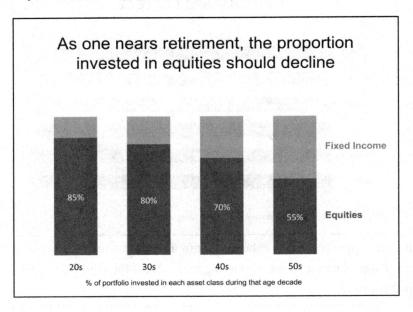

Multiple 100% stacked columns allow you to show how the proportion of one segment changes across regions, time, or another dimension. This visual is similar to the multiple 100% stacked bars and either of these two visuals can be used in similar situations.

Examples of usage:

- showing the split between classes of assets in a portfolio at different age groups
- showing the proportion of sales from a specific product line across sales territories

How to create and use this visual

This visual is created by adding data for multiple categories in the built-in 100% stacked column graph in Excel and PowerPoint. Similar to the single 100% column graph, use colors to indicate the important data and labels instead of legends.

Categorization: Comparing numbers > Components > One vs. total

Multiple 100% diverging stacked bars

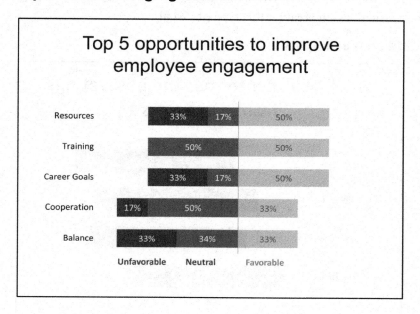

A 100% diverging stacked bar chart positions the bar so part is on each side of a dividing line. This makes it easier to see how the different segments are organized. The dividing line often represents a division between desirable and undesirable results. Multiple categories in the visual allow you to show results from a number of areas or across time. The diverging stacked bar type of chart was described on page 71.

Examples of usage:

- showing the split between favorable and unfavorable responses to a survey conducted in different locations
- showing the proportion of ratings for customer service calls that were above the standard or below the standard across different call centers

How to create and use this visual

Refer to the section on diverging stacked bar charts on page 71 for instructions on creating this type of visual.

Additional examples

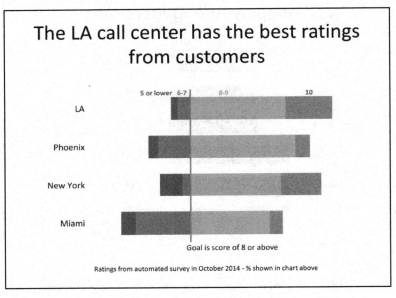

Categorization: Comparing numbers > Components > Explain difference

Sub-group 2: Components explain a difference

Waterfall chart

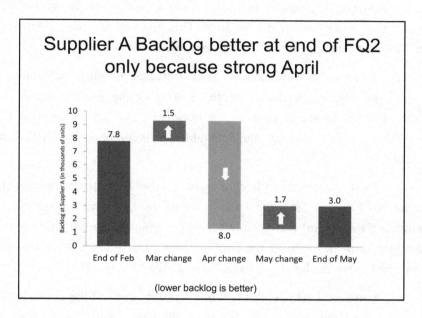

A waterfall graph shows how different components contributed to a movement from a starting value to an ending value. This visual typically shows a column measuring the starting value on the left, a column measuring the ending value on the right, and columns in between showing the components of the difference between the starting and ending values.

Examples of usage:

- showing the components of the change in cash position from the start to the end of the year
- showing the components of the change in a project budget from the start of planning to the end of planning
- showing the components of the change in cost between an accepted industry standard and a new goal

How to create and use this visual

At first glance, it appears that a waterfall graph is hard to create. It is if you have to do the calculations manually. The easiest way to create a waterfall graph is to use a stacked column graph, where one segment is set to No Fill and No Line. This invisible segment "supports" the segment that appears to float above the horizontal axis.

To make the calculations easier, I created an online calculator at www.WaterfallGraphCalculator.com. You enter the starting value and each of the components (positive or negative). The calculator creates a table that you just copy into the data table for the graph in PowerPoint or Excel.

Once the graph has been created, you set the supporting segment to be No Fill and No Line so it is invisible. Clean up the graph by removing the legend and gridlines. If the segments cross the horizontal axis, you will need to set the two segment data series to the same fill color and move the horizontal axis labels to the Low position.

I also suggest you add text box labels to each of the segments so it is easier for the audience to determine the value of that component. If you add these labels, you may remove the vertical axis if doing so will not distort the interpretation of the graph. You can also set the segments to red or green depending on whether they contribute positively or negatively to the ending value. Adding arrows inside the segments can help the audience understand the direction of each segment as seen in the example above.

When presenting this visual, it is often a good idea to use the animation feature to build each component one at a time so you can explain how that component contributed to the change.

Additional examples

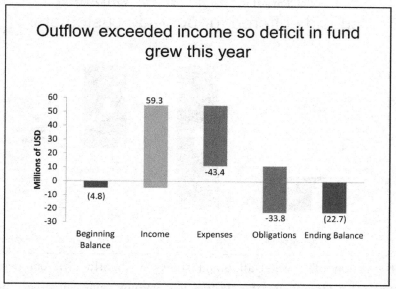

This example uses green and red colors for the segments to indicate whether the amount was favorable or unfavorable to the result.

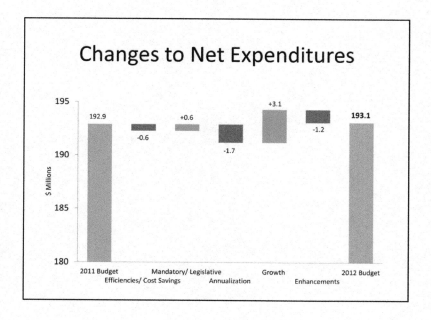

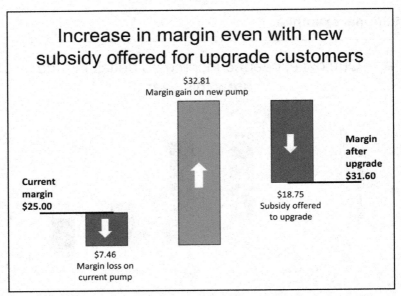

Increase in margin even with new subsidy offered for upgrade customers

$32.81
Margin gain on new pump

Current
margin
$25.00

$7.46
Margin loss on
current pump

Margin
after
upgrade
$31.60

$18.75
Subsidy offered
to upgrade

This version of a waterfall graph shows a slightly different design. Instead of a column for the starting and ending values, lines are used. This works when the focus of the discussion will be on each of the significant changes instead of the starting or ending value.

Steps to a total graph

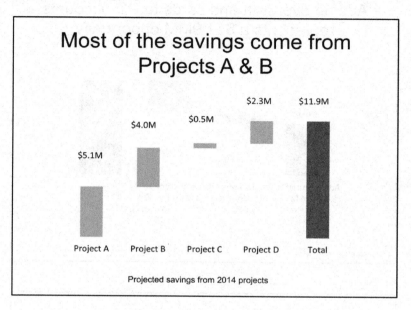

A steps to a total graph shows how components add to a final total. It is similar to a waterfall graph with a starting value of zero.

Examples of usage:

- showing how the cost of the components of a marketing campaign add up to the total budget
- showing how each quarter's results add to the overall result
- showing how cost of the options on an equipment purchase contribute to the total cost

How to create and use this visual

This visual is created using the same technique as the waterfall graph. The starting value is zero and that column is not shown in the graph. Use the steps listed on page 106 for the waterfall graph to create the steps to a total graph.

Additional examples

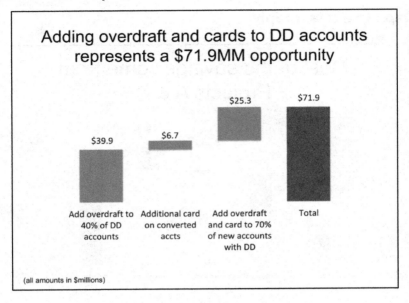

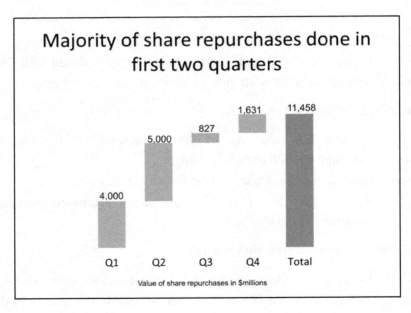

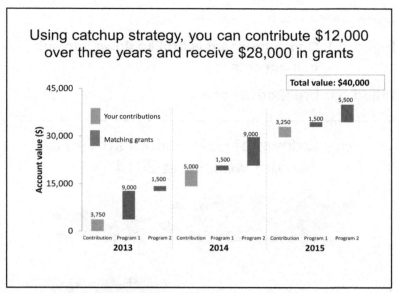

This version of a steps to a total graph shows a slightly different design. Instead of a column for the total value, a callout is used. This was used because of space since there were so many component columns that needed to be included.

Categorization: Comparing numbers > Components > Break down

Sub-group 3: One component is broken down into sub-components

Stacked bar breakdown chart

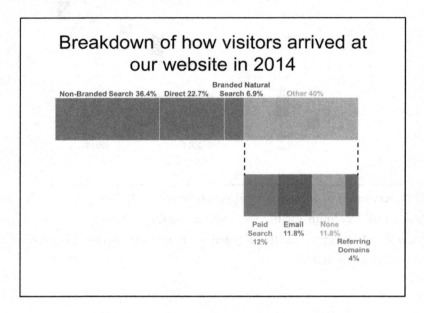

A stacked bar breakdown chart shows how one segment is broken down into sub-segments.

Examples of usage:

- showing how the "Other" category is made up of specific events
- showing how one segment of customers can be further sub-divided to identify the size of an opportunity
- showing how one broad product category can be divided into sub-categories that indicate where marketing focus should be placed

How to create and use this visual

This visual is created using the stacked bar chart in Excel or PowerPoint. Similar to the waterfall graph, the trick is that one segment in the second row is set to be invisible so that the sub-segments appear in the correct position.

In order to make the calculations easier, use the calculator I created at www.StackedBarBreakdownCalculator.com. You enter the segment values, which segment is being broken down, and the sub-segment values. The calculator creates a data table that can be copied into the graph data table for PowerPoint or Excel. The data table includes the spacer segment and the visible segments.

After the stacked bar chart is created, you will need to set the spacer segment to No Fill and No Line so it is invisible. You can then format the chart by removing the legend, both axes, and the gridlines. You can add data labels and text box labels to indicate what each segment represents and the value being represented. I often also manually add dashed lines to connect the top row with the second row so that it is clear which segment is being broken down into sub-segments.

I have also created these visuals by manually calculating the length of rectangles and positioning them beside each other. This can work if the values are very simple and you do not need the power of the calculator.

When presenting this visual, it is often useful to build each segment one by one so that you can tell the story of the data and it is easier for the audience to follow.

Additional examples

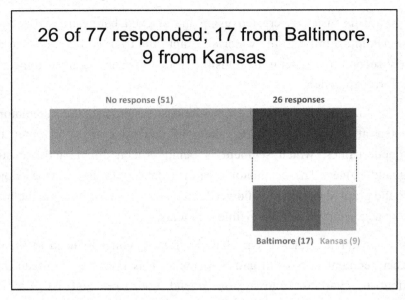

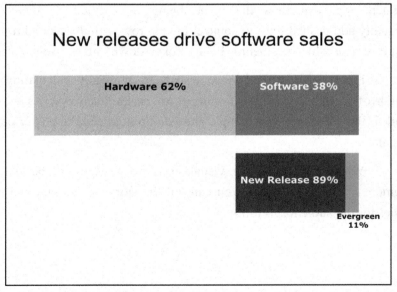

If the segment being broken down is obvious, as in this example, dashed lines are not always needed.

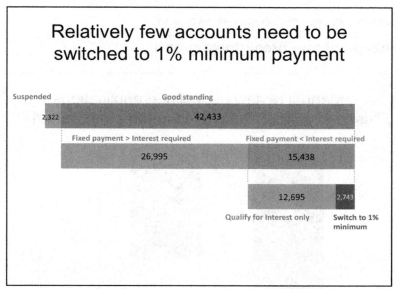

This example shows a second level of breakdown. The green segment breaks down into the gray and orange segments. Then the orange segment breaks down into a gray and red segment. It gives context to the discussion about the accounts in the red segment that need to be switched. If you are using the calculator to create the graph data table, you will have to use it twice in order to get the data for the second level of breakdown.

Categorization: Comparing numbers > Components > Break down

Stacked column breakdown graph

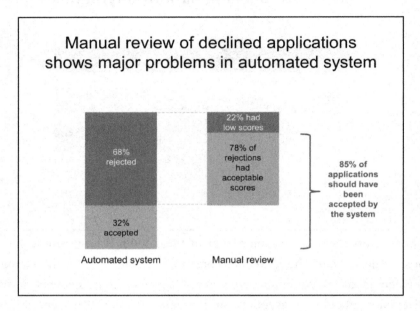

A stacked column breakdown graph shows how one segment is broken down into sub-segments vertically. In most cases, this visual or the stacked bar breakdown chart can be used in similar situations.

Examples of usage:

- showing how the manual review of the results from an automated system indicate problems with the algorithm
- showing how many interviews and offers it took to hire the required number of new staff

How to create and use this visual

This visual is created using the same techniques as on page 113 for the stacked bar breakdown chart. Those techniques are applied to the stacked column graph in Excel or PowerPoint.

Additional examples

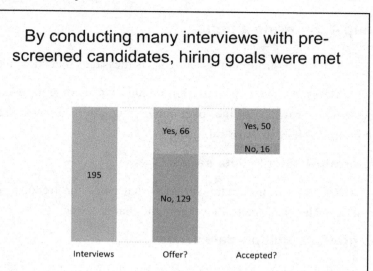

Category 1: Comparing numbers/values/size

Group 4: Showing a trend

The fourth group in this category is messages that show a trend.

Messages in this group often contain words or phrases such as: slope, curve, growth, decline, over time, fluctuation, or over the last x time periods. There are two sub-groups.

Sub-group 1: Single data series

This sub-group contains visuals that show the trend in a single data series. The message is about the trend that is shown.

Sub-group 2: Multiple data series

This sub-group contains visuals that show the trend in more than one data series so that the audience can compare the two trends.

Here is a list of the visuals in this group:

Single data series	Single line graph
	Area graph
Multiple data series	Multiple line graph
	Dual axis line graph

Sub-group 1: Single data series

Single line graph

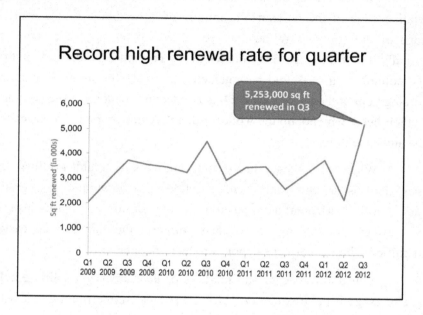

A single line graph shows the trend in values for a single data series.

Examples of usage:

- showing the growth of sales over time
- showing the increase in inventory over time
- showing the rise and fall in expenditures in a department over time
- showing the trend in gas mileage across different average speeds

How to create and use this visual

A line graph is one of the built-in graphs in Excel or PowerPoint. A single line graph uses only one data series in the graph data table.

A column chart should not be used to show a trend. While a column chart can show an increasing or decreasing trend, it does not do it well because the audience becomes confused trying to connect the columns to see the direction or trend of the values. Do they connect the leading edge of the column, the middle of the column, or the trailing edge of the column? While the two edges are the easiest to connect visually, the truth is that the middles of the columns, the hardest spot of the column to use, should be connected to create the trend. If you are forcing your audience to create a line connecting the tops of the columns in their head, why not do the work for them? A line graph is far easier for the audience to understand.

When formatting a line graph, remove any default gridlines, as they can obscure the trend. Make the line thick enough so it is easily seen. On the horizontal axis, position the axis on the tick marks instead of between the tick marks so each point on the line can be easily identified with the correct category on the horizontal axis.

You don't need to add markers or data labels on a line graph. The message is the trend amongst all the points, so interrupting that with markers or numbers makes it harder for the audience to understand the message.

Additional examples

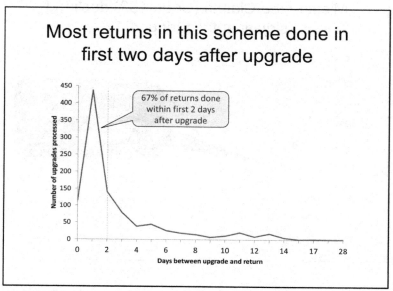

This example uses a callout to draw the audience's attention to one area of the graph.

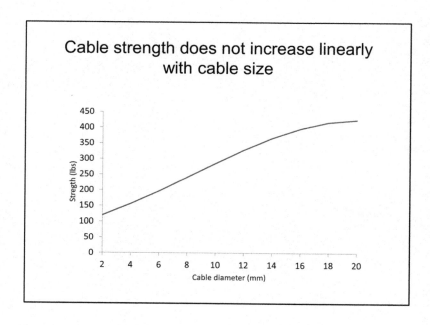

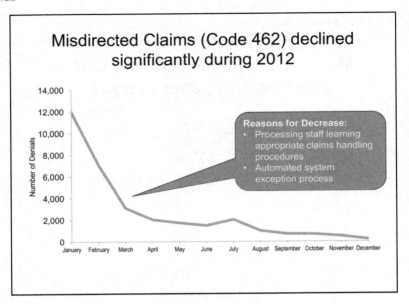

Area graph

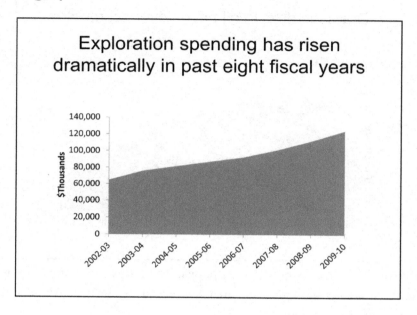

An area graph shows the trend in values for a single data series.

Examples of usage:

* area graphs are used in the same situations as single line graphs

How to create and use this visual

An area graph is one of the built-in graphs in Excel or PowerPoint. It uses only one data series in the graph data table. An area graph can be used instead of a line graph if you want to emphasize the trend. The filled area can be used to add explanatory text about the trend if desired.

As with the other graphs already described, clean up an area graph by removing the gridlines and legend. If you have a lot of data points, reduce the number of categories shown on the horizontal axis so it is easier to understand.

Additional examples

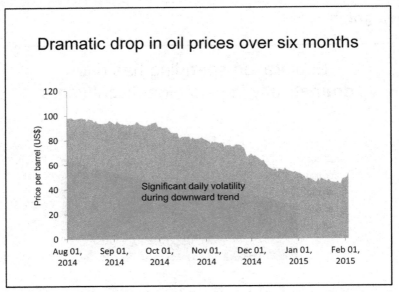

This example uses over 125 data points. The more data points you use the more jagged the top of the area can appear as the lines between the data points get smaller.

Sub-group 2: Multiple data series

Multiple line graph

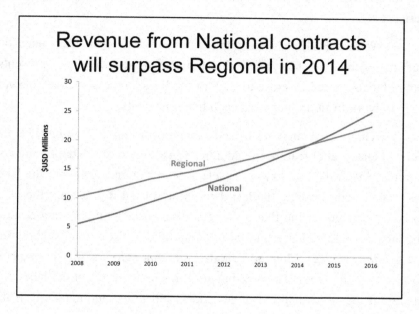

A multiple line graph shows the trend in values for more than one data series. It allows the audience to compare the trend in one data series with the trend in the other data series.

Examples of usage:

- showing the trend in sales of three product lines
- showing the trend in accounts receivables from the top four customers
- showing the trend in stock price of our firm compared to our key competitors and the relevant index

How to create and use this visual

A line graph is one of the built-in graphs in Excel or PowerPoint. A multiple line graph uses more than one data series in the graph data table. As with the single line graph, you will want to clean up the default graph by removing gridlines and making the lines thick enough to easily see. As with other graphs that have multiple data series, use a bold color for the series you want to emphasize and a muted color for the other series.

With a multiple line graph, you will also want to replace the default legend with text labels that indicate what each line represents. These labels should be close to each of the lines so the audience does not have to work to figure out what each line represents.

There are two ways to add labels to the lines. You can use the built-in Data Label feature to add a label just to one of the data points on the line. Select the line first, then select the data point you want the label associated with. Usually the last data point is used if you want the label to be to the right of the lines. You can also select a middle data point if the labels would be better placed in the middle of the graph (as shown in the example above). Then add a data label that contains the series name to just that data point. The advantage of this method is that the label will change if the series name changes and it will move automatically if the graph is moved or resized.

If the data label method will not work, you can use text box labels. Create these labels outside the graph area and then drag them on top of the graph. This way, the labels are not restricted as part of the graph object. If the graph is resized or moved, you will have to move the labels manually.

With either method of adding labels, it is helpful to make the text the same color as the line it is describing. I usually make the text bold as well so it stands out better on the graph. With the color of the line and the label the same, the audience can quickly match the label to the correct line on the graph.

Additional examples

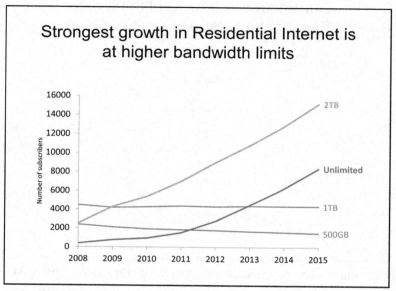

This example shows the use of color to emphasize certain lines.

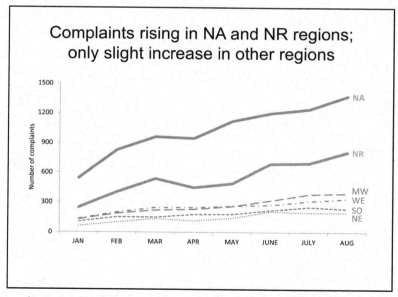

When the muted color is used for less important lines, you may need to use different dashed options to distinguish the lines from each other.

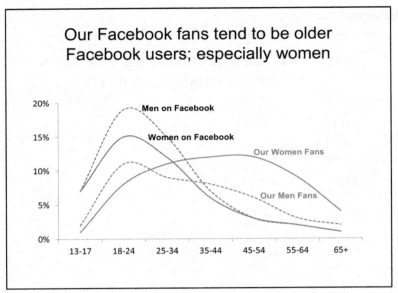

This example uses the feature of smoothing the lines. This gives the trends a more fluid appearance between the data points. Be cautious when using this feature that you do not distort the shape of the trend too much.

Categorization: Comparing numbers > Trend > Multiple data series

Dual axis line graph

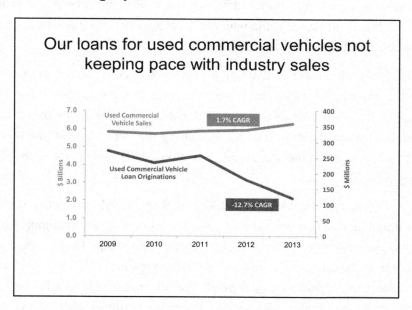

A dual axis line graph shows the correlation or lack of correlation between two trends. Often, the trends are measured using different scales, necessitating the second axis.

Examples of usage:

- showing how sales in an industry are correlated with general economic conditions
- showing how our sales performance is going in an opposite direction to the trend in our industry
- showing how fuel consumption is correlated to speed driven

How to create and use this visual

A dual axis line graph can be created using the built-in line graph in Excel or PowerPoint. It starts as a multiple line graph and one of the data series is set to display on the secondary axis.

As with the line graphs described above, remove gridlines and legends, and make the lines easy to see. Also add text labels to indicate which line represents which data. To assist the audience in knowing which line is measured using which axis, change the color of each axis to the color of the line it is associated with.

Another text box that you may consider adding is a measurement of the trend if that is helpful to the audience. In the example above, the growth rate is shown so the audience can see the difference in the two trends numerically as well as by comparing the lines. As with the labels for each line, make the measurement text boxes the same color as the line they refer to.

One challenge when creating a dual axis graph is deciding on the minimum and maximum values for each vertical axis. By changing these limits, you can make a trend look steeper or less steep. There is no easy answer to the question of how to set these axis limits, but be careful not to distort the appearance of a trend. For all graphs it is usually best to start each measurement axis at zero, but there are times when this would obscure an important trend, so it is not a universal rule to follow.

Don't use a line graph and a column graph in a dual axis graph. Remember that the message is about comparing trends. A trend is best shown using a line, not columns, so use lines for both data series.

There are two situations where a dual axis graph should not be used. First, if the measurement scale for both data series is the same, you should use the previous visual, a multiple line graph. Second, if you are trying to combine two unrelated graphs together to save space on a slide, don't use a dual axis graph; use two graphs to communicate the two messages.

Additional examples

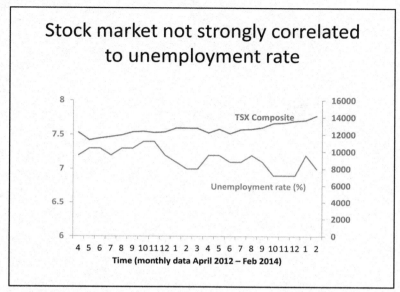

This example uses one axis that does not start at zero. This was done so that the trend in the Unemployment rate could be more easily seen. Make sure you do not manipulate a measurement axis to distort the message. Only change the measurement axis to help the audience see the trend easier.

Category 2: Relationship of sequence

The second category of visuals is the one that shows a sequence visually. Often the sequence may be referred to as a process or flow.

I have organized the visuals in this category into the following groups and sub-groups:

- Linear from start to finish
    - Single path
    - Multiple paths
- Continuous or loop

On the following pages in this chapter, you will see all of the visuals in this category organized by the groups and sub-groups listed above.

Each group will have an introductory page that explains more about the sub-groups for that group and has a list of all of the visuals in that group. At the top of the page for each visual you will see how it is categorized under the category, group, and sub-group. If you need to see a list of all of the visuals in this category, refer to page 21 in the introduction to Step 2.

Category 2: Relationship of sequence

Group 1: Linear from start to finish

The first group in this category is messages that show a linear sequence from a starting point to one or more ending points.

There are two sub-groups.

Sub-group 1: Single path

This sub-group contains visuals that have one starting point and one ending point.

Sub-group 2: Multiple paths

This sub-group contains visuals that have one or more paths between one or more starting and ending points.

Here is a list of the visuals in this group:

Sub-group	Visual
Single path	Chevrons
	Shapes and arrows
	Shapes on an arrow
	Numbered list
Multiple paths	Decision tree
	Parallel paths

Categorization: Sequence > Linear > Single path

Sub-group 1: Single path

Chevrons

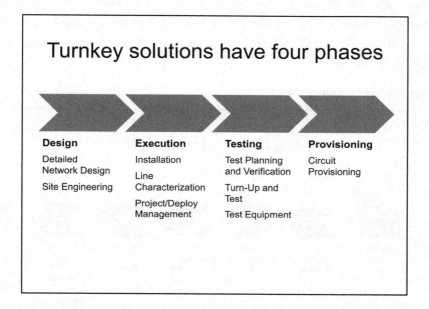

A chevron sequence diagram uses the chevron shape to indicate both a step and the direction to the next step.

Examples of usage:

- steps in a project management process
- steps in a hiring process
- steps in the process for managing documents
- phases in implementing a solution
- steps in setting up a new product

How to create and use this visual

The chevron is a built-in shape in PowerPoint. Draw one chevron for each step in the sequence. Make sure the shapes are the same size. Use the Align and Distribute functions in PowerPoint to make sure the shapes are lined up with each other and are equally distributed in the space you want to use on the slide.

Adding text inside a chevron can sometimes be difficult due to the angles of the shape. Putting explanatory text below the shapes is usually easier. If you want to put text in the chevrons, consider setting the left and right text margins of the shape to zero in order to help the text fit the shape.

Additional examples

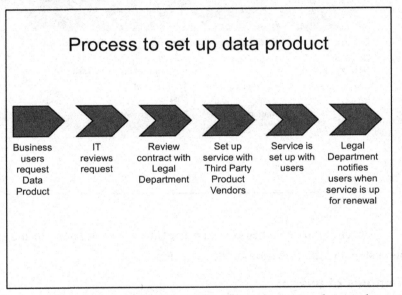

This example uses a pentagon as the first shape to show where the process starts. The pentagon is used because it visually fits with the chevron shape due to the angled sides.

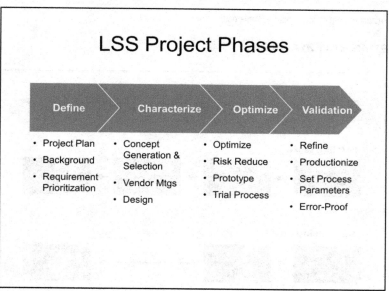

This example shows the chevrons adjacent to each other. When using this arrangement, add an outline to each shape so the audience can distinguish the shapes from each other.

Categorization: Sequence > Linear > Single path

Shapes and arrows

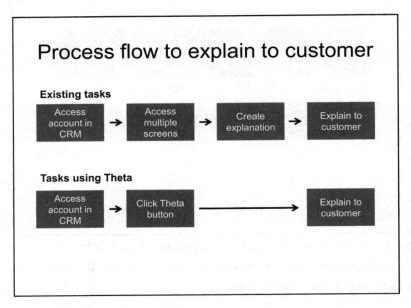

A shapes and arrows sequence diagram uses a shape to indicate a step and an arrow to show the connection to the next step.

Examples of usage:

- showing steps in the process to apply a coating to a vehicle
- showing steps in a system development process
- showing the steps in allocating costs to different cost centers
- showing the steps a customer service rep goes through to resolve an issue

How to create and use this visual

While you can use any of the built-in shapes in PowerPoint, it usually works best to use one of the rectangular shapes. Draw one of the selected shapes for each step in the sequence. Make sure the shapes are the same size. Use the Align and Distribute functions in PowerPoint to make sure the shapes are lined up with each other and are equally distributed in the space you want to use on the slide.

When you add the arrows between the shapes, decide whether the arrows will touch the shapes or not. If they do touch the shapes, it can often be easiest to use the function in PowerPoint that allows you to automatically attach a line to the midpoint of one side of a shape. By attaching the shape and arrow, any time the shape is moved, the line will automatically adjust. If the arrows do not touch the shapes, use the Align function to align the arrows with each other and the midpoint of the shapes.

You can either use the arrow line shape or the block arrows between the shapes. The block arrows are more prominent and may take away from the message unless the movement between steps is also a significant part of the message.

Descriptive text can be added inside or below the shapes. When adding text to a shape, edit the text inside the shape instead of using a separate text box positioned on top of the shape. The text will be easier to automatically position and will move with the shape if it is repositioned.

If you use different shapes to represent different types of steps in the sequence, make sure that you are consistent in using the same shape for the same type of step. This is typical in sequence diagrams that conform to certain drawing standards in an industry or organization.

Instead of shapes, you may consider using images or icons to represent each step. Don't use this if the purpose is strictly decoration. Use images or icons only if they add to the message by describing the step better than just text. You will often also need some descriptive text for each step in addition to the image.

Additional examples

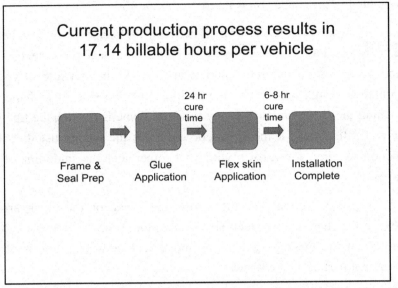

This example shows explanatory text added to the movement between steps.

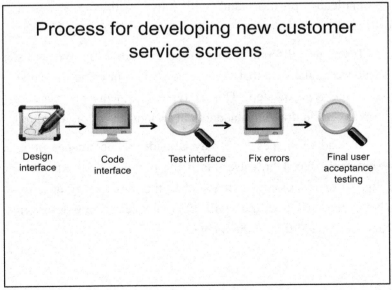

This example shows the use of icons instead of shapes.

Categorization: Sequence > Linear > Single path

Shapes on an arrow

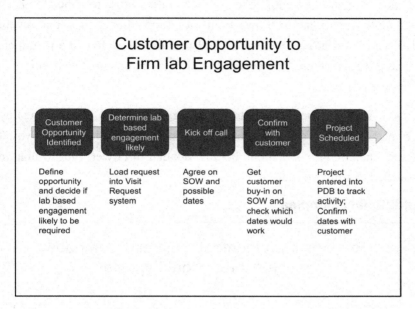

A shapes on an arrow sequence diagram uses a large arrow in the background to show the direction of the sequence and shapes on top of the arrow to indicate each step.

Examples of usage:

- showing steps in the process to deliver ads to a web visitor
- showing steps in developing a new customer service screen in a system
- showing the steps in planning and implementing a financial plan
- showing the steps a customer goes through to contact our company

How to create and use this visual

Start by drawing a large block arrow to cover the area of the slide you want this visual to take up. Since you want the arrow to be a less prominent part of the visual, use a more muted color for it.

On top of the arrow, add shapes to represent each step. A rectangular shape is best if you want to add more than a few words of explanatory text. As with other sequence diagrams, use the Align and Distribute functions in PowerPoint to align the shapes and evenly distribute them along the arrow. Add text inside each shape to indicate the step it represents. You can add additional explanatory text below the shapes if needed.

You may be able to start creating this type of visual by using a pre-made diagram from a site like Diagrammer.com. They offer a variety of sequence diagrams that can be downloaded in PowerPoint format and modified to suit your need.

Additional examples

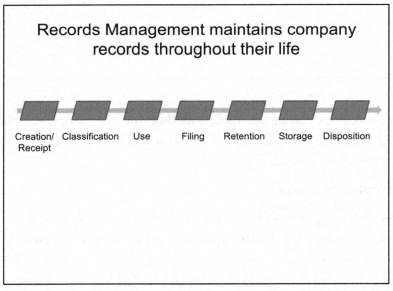

This example shows shapes for each step and descriptions below. If the text will not fit into the shape, put it below the shape.

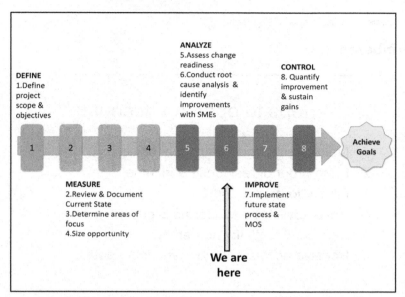

Again, the explanations of each step are placed above or below the shapes due to the length of the required text. The numbers in the shapes indicate the sequence and refer to the related explanations.

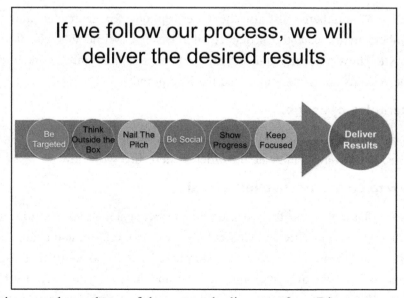

This example used one of the pre-made diagrams from Diagrammer.com as the starting point.

Categorization: Sequence > Linear > Single path

Numbered list

Steps to open an account

1. Make appointment with local office
2. Bring proof of residency & income
3. Fill out forms A1 and C1
4. Have advisor review forms & documents
5. Sign confidentiality agreement
6. Receive account number and login details

A numbered list uses text descriptions for each step and the numbers to indicate the sequence of the steps. While this visual will work to show a linear sequence, my preference is that you use one of the other visuals unless the numbered list is required.

Examples of usage:

- when you want to list the steps in a process
- you want to indicate the order of steps in a workflow

How to create and use this visual

To make sure the list uses the correct spacing and indenting for each step, use the Title and Content layout in PowerPoint and change the bullet type to numbers. Keep the numbered list to no more than eight steps so it is not overwhelming for the audience. If you have a lot of steps, divide them into groups or phases. Present the phases first, then separate slides that list the steps in each phase.

Additional examples

Steps to open an account

1	Make appointment with local office
2	Bring proof of residency & income
3	Fill out forms A1 and C1
4	Have advisor review forms & documents
5	Sign confidentiality agreement
6	Receive account number and login details

This example shows how the numbered list can be improved visually. Instead of the Title and Content layout to keep the spacing correct, this example uses shapes to separate the steps. The shape used in this example is a group of two shapes. The dark rectangle contains the step number, and the lighter rectangle contains the text of the step. By grouping the two shapes, it is easier to move or arrange them. The groups are then Aligned to the left and Distributed evenly across the vertical space.

Categorization: Sequence > Linear > Multiple paths

Sub-group 2: Multiple paths

Decision tree

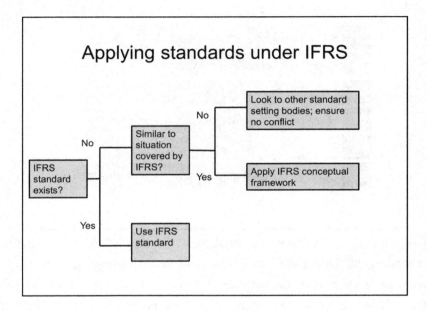

A decision tree diagram shows the questions or decisions that must be made, what the possible answers are, and the outcome of each answer. It helps the audience understand the choices and possible end points you are communicating.

Examples of usage:

- explaining how to decide which process to follow
- showing how to select a product or service that meets the needs
- showing how to select the right equipment for a specific job
- explaining how to decide what standards to use when measuring performance

How to create and use this visual

A decision tree is built in PowerPoint using text boxes and lines. If you want a box around the text for a question or decision, add an outline for that text box instead of using a separate rectangle shape. You can use different fill colors for questions and endpoints if you want to (as shown in the example above).

I find using a connector line is easier than a series of individual line segments to create the lines between the questions that represent each answer path. By linking the connector lines to the midpoint of each of the text box shapes, the lines move automatically if you have to adjust the positioning of the box. Add text box labels to each line so the audience is clear on the answer or decision it represents.

I find using animation to build each path of the decision tree makes it easier to explain when presenting. After you reveal a question, you can take time to explain what considerations go into answering the question. Then you can reveal each answer one at a time, taking time to explain what the answer is, why you would select it, and what the result is if you select that path.

While the typical approach is to explain the decision tree from the left to the right, you can also use it in the reverse direction. You would do this when your message is to show how we ended up at a particular end point and what decisions were made to arrive at that point. You can also discuss the alternative decisions that could have been taken at certain points along the path.

If your decision tree is too complex or too crowded on the slide, break it up into phases that you can explain on separate slides. You can do this in one of two ways. First, you can summarize the decision tree into higher level groups, explain the overall relationships, then proceed to explain one slide for each group in the overall diagram. Second, you can create a series of slides for each path possible. Your first slide shows the first key decision that needs to be made and the possible outcomes.

Subsequent slides show the next level along each path. Come back to the previous level when necessary so the audience isn't lost during the explanation.

Additional examples

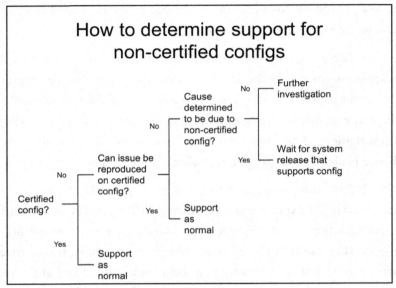

This example does not use boxes around each question or endpoint. It can give a less cluttered look if there are more steps in the decision tree.

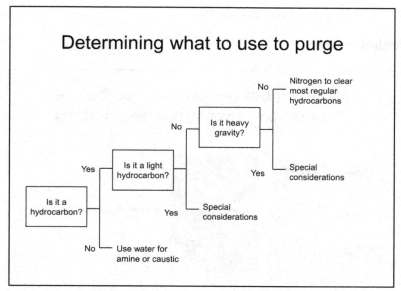

This example uses boxes only for the questions, not the endpoints.

This example uses a minimalist approach to the lines.

Categorization: Sequence > Linear > Multiple paths

Parallel paths

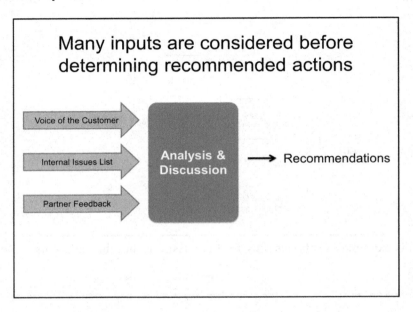

A parallel paths diagram shows a sequence where there are steps being done at the same time as other steps before the end is reached.

Examples of usage:

- showing how many inputs are gathered at the same time before an analysis phase
- showing how multiple steps must be taken to allocate the different components of one amount to the different accounts
- showing how different steps are taken depending on what model of equipment is installed

How to create and use this visual

A parallel path diagram is constructed similar to a single path linear sequence diagram as discussed starting on page 138. When necessary, use the Align and Distribute functions to make the parallel lines or shapes properly positioned.

Additional examples

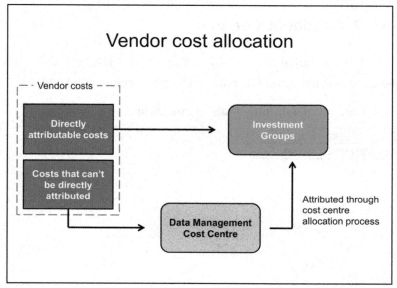

This example shows two portions of costs from a vendor that are treated differently when allocating costs.

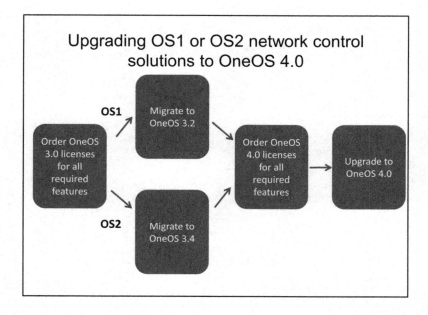

Category 2: Relationship of sequence

Group 2: Continuous or loop

The second group in this category is messages that show a sequence that starts again once the last step has been completed.

Here is a list of the visuals in this group:

Circle and shapes
Shapes and circular arrows

Circle and shapes

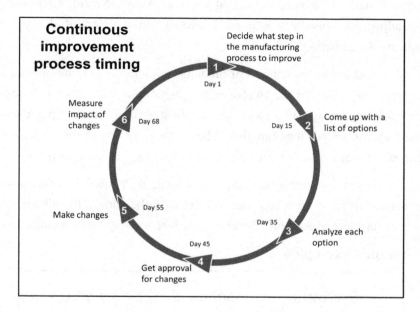

A circle and shapes diagram uses a circle to indicate the continuous flow direction and shapes on top of the circle to describe each step.

Examples of usage:

- showing the steps in a continuous improvement process
- showing the steps in refining a final output through a series of cycles

How to create and use this visual

A circle and shapes diagram is created by first drawing a circle or circular arrow shape as large as you need it to be on the slide. If you are using a circle, set the fill color to None and use the thickness of the outline to create the circle. You may want to add a shape, like a triangle, to indicate the direction of the cycle. If you are using a circular block arrow, set the fill color to a muted color so it does not draw attention away from the steps of the process. Use the adjustment handles to make the circular arrow narrower or wider as needed. You can also use a proportionally drawn arc shape that you can extend to a full circle using the adjustment handles. Add an arrowhead to the end of the arc to indicate the direction of the cycle.

Add the shapes on top of the underlying circle, adding one shape for each step. Start at the twelve noon position so the audience follows the cycle as they would a clock. As demonstrated in the example above, you may use shapes that can also indicate the direction of the cycle. Add text to the shape or around the shape to further explain each step.

When presenting this type of visual, it is often helpful to use animation to bring each step one at a time on the slide. This allows you to give further explanation of each step before moving on to the next one.

Additional examples

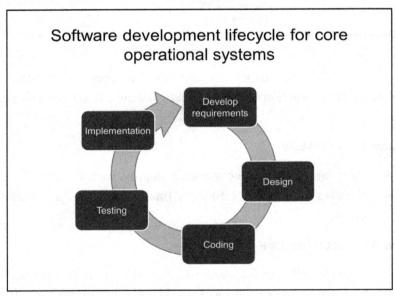

This example uses a circular block arrow to show the direction of the cycle and rectangles to show each step.

Shapes and circular arrows

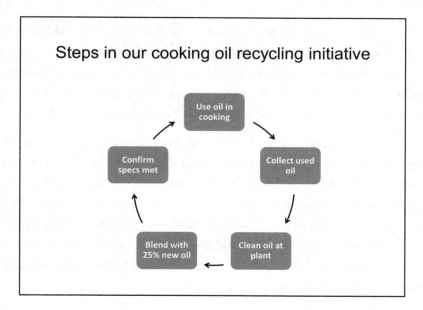

A shapes and circular arrows diagram uses arrows to show the flow between the steps. The cycle is continuous because an arrow indicates that after the last step, the cycle continues by returning to the first step.

Examples of usage:

- showing the steps in a recycling process
- showing the steps in the cycle of continuously improving the skills of a factory

How to create and use this visual

There are four ways to create the type of visual in PowerPoint.

First, you can use the SmartArt feature of PowerPoint and use one of the built-in the Cycle diagram styles. While this does make it easier to create the diagram initially, SmartArt limits the flexibility you have in repositioning and formatting the diagram. If one of the style options is acceptable, you can use this method. The example above is a SmartArt diagram.

The second method is related to the first. If the built-in SmartArt cycle diagram styles won't fit your need, but one of them is close to what you want to create, you may be able to use the SmartArt as the starting point. You can convert the SmartArt diagram to a drawing, then Ungroup the individual elements. Now you have full control over every shape.

If you want to have full control from the start, you can use the third method and create your own cycle diagram using shapes and arc lines. Start by drawing the shapes that you need to represent each step and positioning them in an approximate circle. It is important to move the first shape (which should be at the twelve noon location) and the next clockwise shape very close to their final positions on the slide. You can also use images or icons instead of shapes if that will be more effective in communicating each step to the audience.

Draw a proportional arc shape (hold the Shift key down while drawing the arc) that connects the middle of the shapes at twelve noon and the next clockwise shape. This will define the circle that the shapes will ultimately be aligned on. Adjust the start and end of the arc using the adjustment handles, make the line thicker if desired, and add an arrowhead to the end of the arc to create a curved arrow shape. To maintain the perfect circle alignment, copy and paste the arc shape and align the copy on top of the original. Then use the adjustment handles of the copy to move the start and end points to where they need to be to show the movement to the next shape. Continue this process until all the arcs have been created. You may end up slightly repositioning the shapes so they fit properly between the arcs.

The fourth method for creating a shapes and circular arrows diagram is to modify a pre-made diagram you download from a site like Diagrammer.com. You can select the number of steps in the cycle and the style of diagram you like. Once it is downloaded in PowerPoint format, customize it as needed.

Additional examples

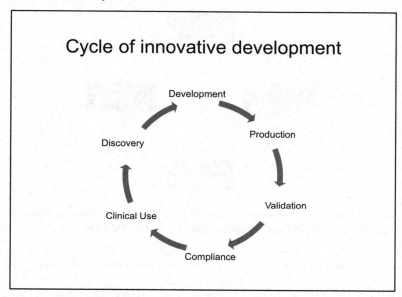

This example is a SmartArt diagram that was converted and Ungrouped in order to customize it.

(examples continue on next page)

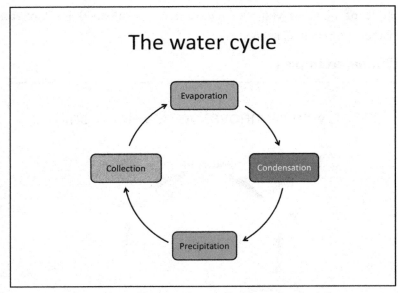

This example is drawn using the shapes and arcs method.

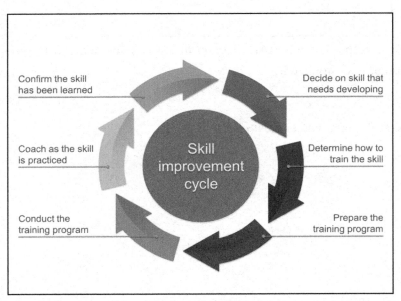

This example starts with a diagram from Diagrammer.com and has been customized.

Category 3: Relationship over time

The third category of visuals is the one that shows a relationship over a time period.

I have organized the visuals in this category into the following groups:

- Duration of events is shown
- Only when event occurs is shown

On the following pages in this chapter, you will see all of the visuals in this category organized by the groups listed above.

Each group will have an introductory page that has a list of all of the visuals in that group. At the top of the page for each visual you will see how it is categorized under the category, and group. If you need to see a list of all of the visuals in this category, refer to page 21 in the introduction to Step 2.

Category 3: Relationship over time

Group 1: Duration of events is shown

The first group in this category is messages that need to show the duration of each event in addition to when the event occurs.

Here is a list of the visuals in this group:

Gantt chart
Calendar with duration shapes

Categorization: Time > Duration shown

Gantt chart

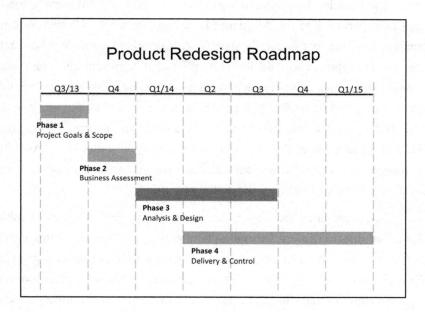

A Gantt chart shows the duration of each task using the length of each bar, and the positioning of the bar indicates when the task takes place during the time period.

Examples of usage:

- when you want to show the schedule of tasks along a timeline
- when you want to show how long each task will take in a project in addition to when each task starts and ends

How to create and use this visual

A Gantt chart can be created in project management software and exported as an image to be included on your slide. Be careful about using these exported images as they can often be cluttered and may confuse the audience because of the distracting elements.

You can also create a Gantt chart using PowerPoint shapes and position the bars in approximately the correct position along the timeline. Create the timeline first using a horizontal line and vertical lines to mark each time period. Use the Align and Distribute features of PowerPoint to create a timeline that is evenly spaced. Add labels to indicate what each time period represents. Add the rectangles that represent each task and position them approximately where they should be. This type of visual, while it may not be perfectly accurate, is easier to understand and can be built bar by bar using the PowerPoint animation feature. Limit your Gantt chart to eight or fewer bars to keep it easy to understand. As with an image exported from project management software, you don't want the clutter to be confusing to the audience.

A more accurate way to create a Gantt chart is to use a table (Julie Terberg of Terberg Design is the one who told me about this idea). Create a table that has 4 or 5 columns for each time period you want to show (ie. if you want to show 5 months, create a table with 25 columns). You can draw borders in the table to delineate each of the time periods. To create a bar of the correct length, select the correct number of columns and set the fill color for those table cells to a visible color. By dividing each time period into five segments, it allows you to create a bar that starts part way through a time period, finishes part way through a time period, or lasts only a portion of a time period. This method makes it easy to change the length or position of any bar more accurately than just moving it by best guess manually.

Additional examples

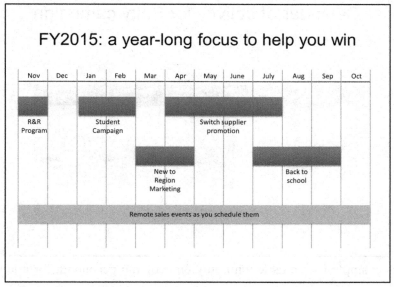

This example shows how text that will not fit into the rectangle can be placed below the shape.

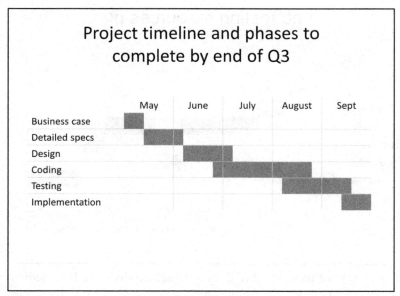

This example uses the table method of creating the Gantt chart.

Calendar of activity for Salty campaign

			2016										
Channel	Jan	Feb	Mar	April	May	June	July	Aug	Sept	Oct	Nov	Dec
Retail Activity	Execute Retail Contest				Ads promoting launch of Salty Season at MD							
On Premise Activity	Execute On-Premise Contest		Contest Finalists are selected		Salty Program Launch			Contest Winner Party	Fall Seasonal Salty Program		Winter Seasonal Salty Program	

This example uses a table with only one column per month for a longer project.

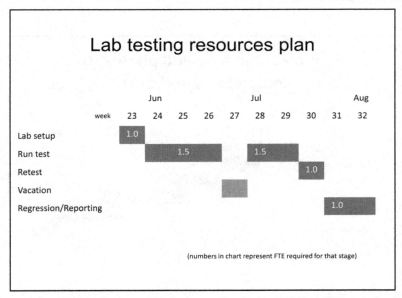

Lab testing resources plan

	week	23	24	25	26	27	28	29	30	31	32
		Jun					Jul				Aug
Lab setup		1.0									
Run test			1.5				1.5				
Retest									1.0		
Vacation											
Regression/Reporting										1.0	

(numbers in chart represent FTE required for that stage)

This example of using a table does not include dividing lines and works best when the bars are not on top of one another.

Calendar with duration shapes

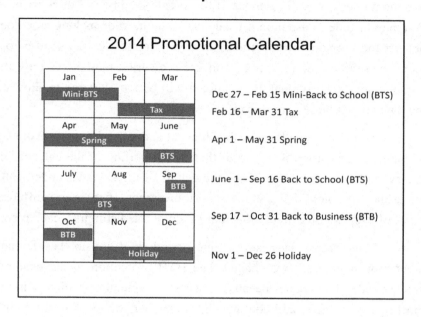

A calendar with duration shapes shows the duration of each task using the length of each bar, and the positioning of the bar indicates when the task takes place during the time period represented by the calendar.

Examples of usage:

- showing when promotions are planned during the next fiscal year
- showing when key tasks in the project take place during the next two months

How to create and use this visual

The first step is to create the calendar. There is no built-in calendar feature in PowerPoint, so the calendar is created using a table. Create a table in PowerPoint with the correct number of rows and columns for the time period you need to show.

If all of the dates are within a single month, use a monthly calendar that shows all of the days of that month like you would see in a one month desk or wall calendar. If the events span two or three months, you may be able to use monthly calendars on one slide as long as it does not get too crowded on the slide. Once you get events that span across more than three months it is best to use a diagram that shows only the months, not the individual days, since it will be too cluttered to show all the days in that large a time span.

To indicate the length of each event and when it happens, draw a rectangle and position it on top of the correct portion of the calendar. If you want the audience to still see the details of the calendar underneath, make the fill color of the shape semi-transparent. If there are different types of events, you can use different fill colors to distinguish each type.

If an event spans across time periods that are not beside each other, you may need two shapes. The BTB promotion in the example above needed two shapes because it starts in September, which is in the third row of months, and continues into October, which is in the fourth row of months.

Additional examples

Key project steps in next 2 months

January						
S	M	T	W	T	F	S
		1	2	3	4	5
6	7	8	9	10	11	12
13	14	15	16	17	18	19
20	Bus decisions, Product Specs, Ops Impact assessment				26	
27	ACME mapping JAD, Circuit & Security ☆					

SC update

February						
S	M	T	W	T	F	S
					1	2
3	Finalize arch, infr, dev; Prep for ACME contract signing					9
10	WBS; Gate 1 previews					16
17	18	☆ 19 SC Gate 1 presn	20	21	22	23
24	25	26	27	☆ 28 Sign ACME contract		

This example shows a more detailed calendar and the need to use semi-transparent shapes when covering up part of the calendar.

Category 3: Relationship over time

Group 2: Only when event occurs is shown

The second group in this category is messages that only need to show when the event occurs during the time period.

Here is a list of the visuals in this group:

Simple timeline
Calendar with event indicators

Categorization: Time > Only when event occurs

Simple timeline

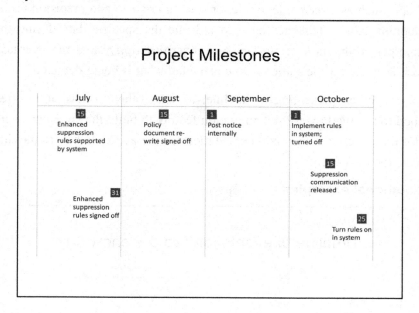

A simple timeline uses shapes to indicate when each task takes place during the time period.

Examples of usage:

- showing when key communication will happen during a project
- showing key dates related to dividend payment during the fiscal year
- showing key milestone dates in a project
- showing the timeline of key tasks for getting social media posts out during the weeks

How to create and use this visual

The timeline for this visual is created using the same techniques of aligning and distributing horizontal and vertical lines as the first method for creating a Gantt chart described on page 162.

For each task or event, add a shape that indicates when that task occurs during the time period depicted by the timeline. It can be any shape, such as a rectangle, circle, or star. In order to add precision to the diagram, add text in the shape to indicate the specific date during the time period this task occurs on. Add other descriptive text for each task so it is easier for the audience to understand what is being depicted.

When presenting a timeline, as with other visuals, it is often good to use the PowerPoint animation feature to build the slide one event at a time. You can then add explanation for the audience before moving on to the next event.

Additional examples

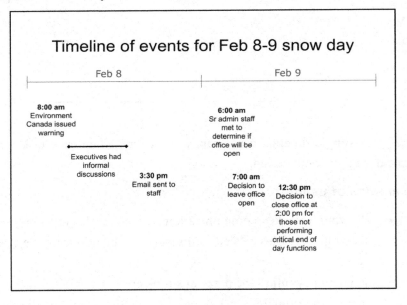

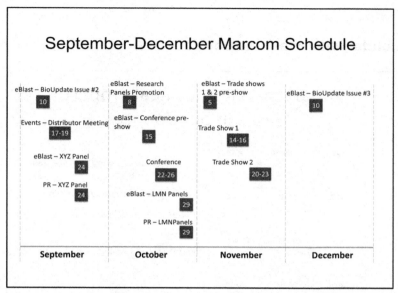

This example shows staggering the text and shapes in case room is tight on the timeline. It also shows the timeline on the bottom of the visual.

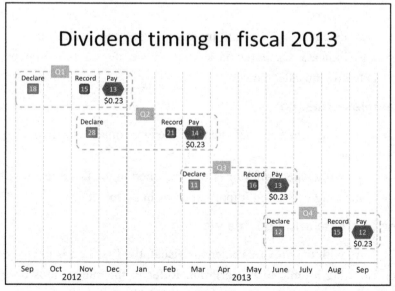

This example uses different colors to indicate the three types of events depicted in the timeline and uses a dashed line to group related events.

Categorization: Time > Only when event occurs

Calendar with event indicators

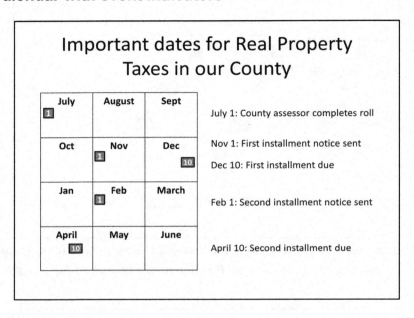

A calendar with event indicators uses the positioning of the shapes to indicate when the task takes place during the time period represented by the calendar.

Examples of usage:

- showing when special events at the city square happen during the year
- showing when milestones were reached in the last three months
- showing upcoming important dates in a project

How to create and use this visual

As with the previous calendar visual, the first step is to create the calendar using a table in PowerPoint. Refer to the suggestions on page 165 for creating the calendar.

Once the calendar is created, you can add shapes to indicate each event or task. Use the suggestions on page 170 in the simple timeline visual to create these shapes and the accompanying explanatory text.

As with the simple timeline and other visuals, building the diagram one event at a time focuses the audience on each event as it is introduced and explained.

Additional examples

4 workshops scheduled in July

Sun	Mon	Tue	Wed	Thu	Fri	Sat
1	2	3	4	5	☆ 6 Data	7
8	☆ 9 Data	10	11	12	13	14
15	16	17	18	19	20	21
22	23	24	★ 25 Integration	★ 26	27	28
29	30	31				

If you want to use one shape for different types of events, use a different color for each type of event, as shown in this example.

(examples continue on next page)

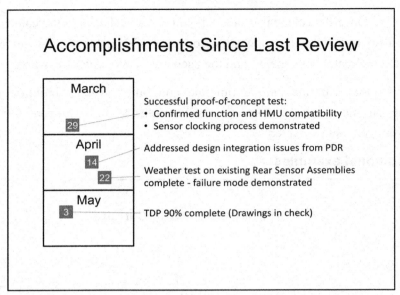

By positioning the calendar on one side of the slide, this example allows for more explanatory text for each event.

Timeline for AP / AR Process

Nov 9	10	11	12 Impact Meeting	13 Promote Changes	14 Change Approval	15
16	17	18	19	20	21	22
23	24	25	26 User Training	27 User Training	28	29
30	Dec 1	2	3 Release Forms	4 Go Live	5	6
7	8	9	10		12	13

This example shows text used for all events except the most important event, which uses a shape to make it stand out.

Category 4: Relationship between entities

The fourth category of visuals is the one that shows a relationship between entities.

I have organized the visuals in this category into the following groups:

- Hierarchical relationship
- Geographic relationship
- Comparison
- Mathematical relationship
- Group of items

On the following pages in this chapter, you will see all of the visuals in this category organized by the groups listed above.

Each group will have an introductory page that has a list of all of the visuals in that group. At the top of the page for each visual you will see how it is categorized under the category, and group. If you need to see a list of all of the visuals in this category, refer to page 21 in the introduction to Step 2.

Category 4: Relationship between entities

Group 1: Hierarchical relationship

The first group in this category is messages where the relationship between the items is hierarchical.

Here is a list of the visuals in this group:

Bullet point list
Organizational chart
Breakdown diagram

Bullet point list

Critical Success Factors this year

- Control input costs
- Establish new markets for products
- Raise productivity by 1%
- Push R&D efforts:
  - User interface
  - Functionality

A bullet point list is used to break down a higher level topic, usually the slide headline, into sub-topics.

Examples of usage:

- showing the list of key projects for the quarter
- showing the items in the meeting agenda

How to create and use this visual

While the bullet list slide is very common, it is not because presenters have made a conscious decision that this visual is the correct one for their message. It is because this is the default slide layout in PowerPoint. A bullet point list should only be used where a hierarchical relationship exists between the headline of the slide and the points below. If you do use a bullet point list, use the default layout in PowerPoint so that the positioning and spacing is consistent for each bullet and each slide.

Additional examples

Agenda

- Review of past action items
- Discussion of current results
- Presentation of proposed initiatives
- Decisions on priorities for next quarter
- Decision on next meeting location & date

Categorization: Entities > Hierarchical

Organizational chart

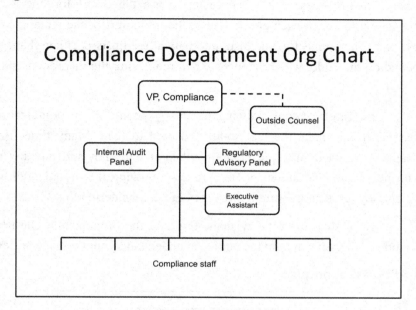

An organizational chart illustrates the relationship of different levels of employees in an organization. A direct reporting relationship is indicated by a solid line and an indirect reporting relationship is indicated by a dashed line.

Examples of usage:

- to show the different levels in an organization
- to show who reports to whom in a department
- to show which employees should be contacted about which client issues
- to show the reporting relationship of project team members

How to create and use this visual

PowerPoint has an organizational chart diagram as part of the SmartArt feature, but I find it is not flexible enough. I suggest you create this visual using rectangles, text boxes, and lines. That way, you can create the exact diagram you want. If you use rectangles, add the text as part of the shape so it moves with the shape if the shape is repositioned. When drawing lines, it is often easier to use the connector line as it allows you to attach each end to one of the midpoints of the rectangle or text box. The connector line also automatically adjusts if either shape is moved on the slide, which happens when modifying the diagram as staff change.

Be careful about showing too many people in an organization chart as it can make the text small and hard to read. Many times this visual is included in a presentation when it does not add any useful information for the audience. Be sure that showing the organization of the employees is an important message before considering this visual.

As with many other visuals, building the organization chart by person or by level can help the audience understand your message easier.

Additional examples

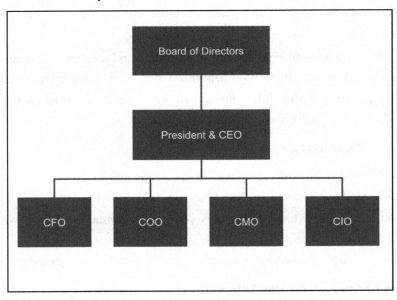

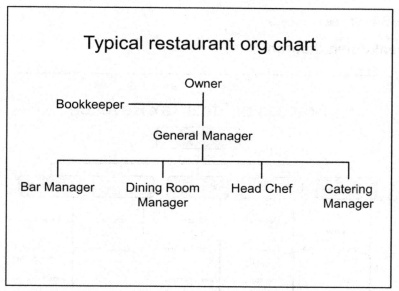

This example does not use a rectangle for each role, just the text describing that role. It gives a cleaner, more modern look to the visual.

Categorization: Entities > Hierarchical

Breakdown diagram

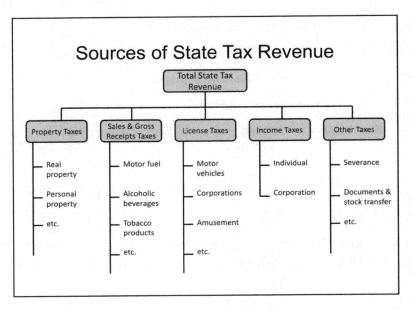

A breakdown diagram shows the hierarchy from macro level items at the top, to more micro level items at the bottom. The lines show how a higher level item breaks down into component items below it.

Examples of usage:

- breaking down a large topic into sub-topics
- showing the components of a larger topic
- showing the sub-tasks of a section of a project

How to create and use this visual

A breakdown diagram is created using rectangles, text boxes, and shapes, just like an organization chart described on page 179. It is very similar to an organization chart, the difference being that it does not describe reporting relationships within an organization. It describes breakdown of items or ideas.

Category 4: Relationship between entities

Group 2: Geographic relationship

The second group in this category is messages where the relationship between the items is based on location geographically.

Here is a list of the visuals in this group:

Map

Map

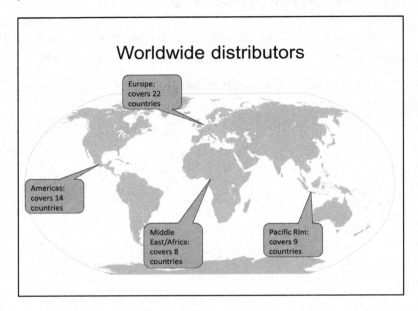

This visual shows the relationship between the entities by locating them on a map of the overall area.

Examples of usage:

- you want to show where events take place on a map
- you want to show where each sales territory is
- you want to show where your retail locations are compared to the competition
- you want to point out the features of a property on a site map

How to create and use this visual

When using a map, make sure it is a high resolution image that will not be fuzzy when the audience views it. If possible, try to find a map that has a transparent background so that the map does not appear in a white rectangle. This will likely be a PNG file since the PNG file format supports transparency. Make sure you have permission to use the map image. Either purchase the map image or find one that allows commercial use in the license.

You can use many different ways to place information on a map. You can use simple text or callouts as shown in the example above. You can also show values using proportional shapes placed in each region on the map. You could use photos to show the company stores in each city in the state. And there are many more ways to represent the information on a map. Make sure that the visual you are using for each location is accurately placed on the map.

Additional examples

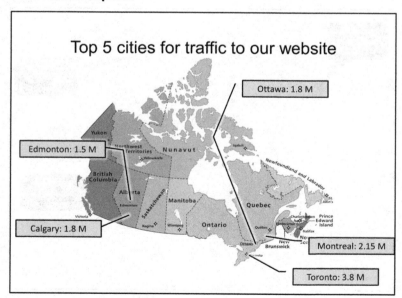

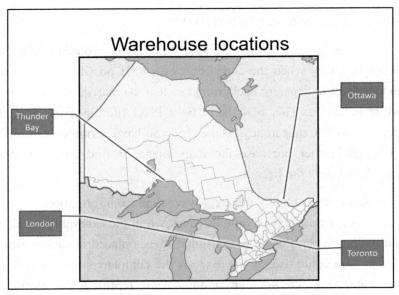

This example, and the previous one, show the benefit of using callouts to point out specific locations on the map.

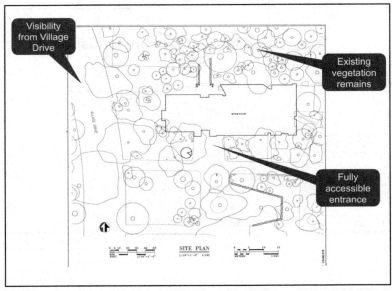

This example shows a site plan, which is another type of map visual.

Category 4: Relationship between entities

Group 3: Comparison

The third group in this category is messages where the relationship is comparing items on different criteria.

Here is a list of the visuals in this group:

Table

Table

Options for addressing inventory system issues in 2015

	Add On	New Product	New Platform
Cost	Low	Moderate	High + annual fees
Functionality	Minimal	Moderate	Full
Time to Market	Quick	Medium	Long
Customer Experience	Poor	Improved	Optimal
Employee Experience	Poor	Improved	Excellent
Future capabilities	None	Minimal	Complete

A table allows the audience to quickly see how each option measures against the same set of criteria.

Examples of usage:

- you have a set of criteria that you are evaluating different options against
- you want to compare your product against competing products
- you want to show what is included or not included in different service levels

How to create and use this visual

A table can be oriented vertically or horizontally. A vertical table has the criteria in rows in the first, or left most, column. Each subsequent column represents one of the items or options and the cells in that column indicate how that item measures on the criteria for each row. A horizontal table has the criteria in columns in the top row. Each row below represents one of the items or options and the cells in that row indicate how that item measure on the criteria for each column.

You can create a table using the PowerPoint Table feature. When using the built-in PowerPoint tables, change the default format that has many shades of colors to a format that is clean and simple. You can also create a table using a text box in PowerPoint. In the text box, you can use tabs to create the columns.

You can also copy a table of Excel cells into PowerPoint. There are many options for copying Excel cells into PowerPoint. If you want to use the Excel cells as a PowerPoint table so you have all the PowerPoint formatting options, you can use the simple Copy and Paste method. There are other methods that allow you to paste the cells as an image, link to the Excel file, or embed the Excel file into the PowerPoint file. These methods all have advantages and disadvantages. You can find more information about these options on my website at http://paradi.link/ExcelInPowerPoint.

Additional examples

When to recommend Private Network vs. Shared Network Services

	Private Network	Shared Network Services
Technical experience	In-house	Limited & staff don't have time to learn
Cabling availability	12-24 mo. ROI for new cabling	No spare cables available
Budgeting approach	CAPEX	Outsource & OPEX
Bandwidth requirements	Unpredictable; easy upgrade from 10G to 100G	Minimal growth expected
Maintenance approach	Flexibility, quick response time	Prefer service provider to maintain network

We address the special needs of large families in a way no one else can

		Large Financial Services Institution	Small Independent Firms	ABC Co.
People	Specialized Talent	✓		✓
	Backups to key staff	✓		✓
	Intellectual Capital	✓		✓
Products/ Services	Conflict Free		✓	✓
	Broad set of products	✓	✓	✓
	Open Architecture		✓	✓
Structure/ Culture	Stability & Durability	✓		✓
	Focused Business		✓	✓
	Employee Owned		✓	✓
	Boutique Feel		✓	✓

This example uses checkmarks to indicate whether the criteria is met or not. ABC Co. used this visual to show how they addressed all the needs.

Observers required in Phase 1 so they can fully participate in phase 2

Core Team Role	Resource Name	Phase 1		Phase 2	
		Observer	Participate	Observer	Participate
BPE resource	Lillian Craig		✓		✓
BPM IT Analyst	Tim Hampton		✓		✓
Business Solutions Lead	Darryl Wright		✓		✓
IT Architecture Lead	Garry Moore	✓			✓
Service Channel	Connie Austin	✓			✓
Consumer Engagement	Israel Houston	✓			✓
Information Management	Renee Watson	✓			✓

Maryann Young as Business Owner approves both phases
Xuan Vincent as Requirements Lead is accountable for both phases

You can also use a simple design without color as shown in this example.

Category 4: Relationship between entities

Group 4: Mathematical relationship

The fourth group in this category is messages where the relationship between the items is mathematical.

Here is a list of the visuals in this group:

Equation diagram
Calculation

Categorization: Entities > Mathematical

Equation diagram

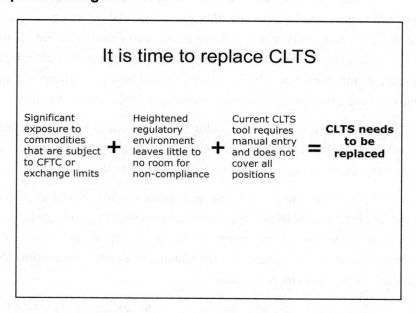

An equation diagram uses elementary school math concepts and visual arrangements to show how a conclusion is reached by adding up arguments or reasons.

Examples of usage:

- you want to persuade a decision maker to approve a project
- you want the audience to agree with your reasoning for making a decision
- you want to convince the audience to support an initiative

How to create and use this visual

An equation diagram is created using text boxes and a line. If the diagram is horizontally oriented, the text boxes and operators (such as the + sign) are usually aligned at the midpoint of each element. If the diagram is oriented vertically, the text within each text box is often right aligned, as numbers would be in a mathematical equation. There is a line below all the arguments and the conclusion text box is below the line.

This visual benefits from being presented one argument at a time by using the animation feature of PowerPoint. It allows the presenter to more fully explain each item and how they add up to the conclusion.

This visual can be effective as a summary or call to action slide at the end of a presentation. It allows the presenter to reinforce the key messages made during the body of the presentation and leaves the audience with a compelling visual statement of the conclusion the presenter wants them to understand.

This visual can also be used as an agenda slide during a persuasive presentation. It clearly outlines the items the presenter will be covering and how they lead to the conclusion the presenter hopes the audience reaches at the end. Using this visual at both the start and end of the presentation can be very effective.

Additional examples

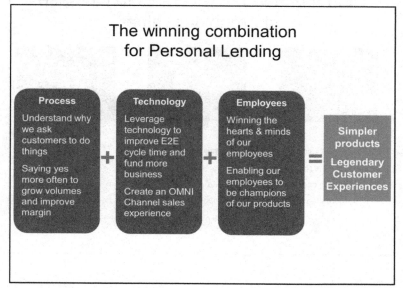

When there is more text, putting it inside a shape can help the audience distinguish the groups from each other, as this example shows.

Approving water & sewer infrastructure projects benefits residents

Create jobs and economic development

\+   Stewardship of the environment

\+   Improve health & safety for residents
_____
Increase in quality of life for residents

This example could be used as an agenda slide to make clear the arguments you will use to lead the audience to the desired conclusion.

Help manage fee reversals to increase shareholder value

How you can help manage fee reversals:

Address the root cause

Ensure the customer is in the right plan

Promote the value add features and benefits

Calculation

FY2015 summary of baggage fee revenue

Revenue from second bag fees	$568,893
Lost revenue from elite level fees waived	-$47,239
Revenue from overweight bag fees	$585,805
Total net baggage revenue	**$1,107,459**

A calculation diagram shows how a final value is calculated so the audience understands the components that go into the final value.

Examples of usage:

- when you need to show how an assumption was calculated
- when you want to explain how a fee is calculated based on different inputs
- showing how the cost of different phases add to the total cost

How to create and use this visual

A calculation diagram is constructed similar to an equation diagram described on page 194. Use the text boxes and line to show each component of the calculation. Use the Align tools to line up the text boxes for the components and the operators. Like an equation diagram, a calculation diagram can be vertically or horizontally oriented. When using a text box for numbers, use the Decimal Tab to align the numbers properly in a column. The text in this visual is usually not put inside a shape because you want it to look like an equation the audience will be familiar with from their days in school.

Additional examples

Derivation of		
Investment Return Assumptions		
Inflation	2.5%	assumption
Real return	+ 4.1%	70% probability of achieving
Pre-tax return	6.6%	
Less taxes	-1.5%	assumes 22% tax rate
After-tax return	**5.1%**	

Insurance Allocation Overview

In-service property
insurance rate for the
building

X

Insurable value
of building

=

Insurance
premium for
building

*(combines third party
coverage with Realty
premiums and is weighted due
to risk factors of the building)*

Utilize market benchmarking data (BOMA & IREM) and input from our national
insurance brokers to keep premiums within market

This example shows a calculation that uses descriptions of the values instead of numbers.

Category 4: Relationship between entities

Group 5: Group of items

The fourth group in this category is messages that show a group of related items.

Here is a list of the visuals in this group:

Text points
Text in shapes

Categorization: Entities > Group of items

Text points

Product features

New slim design

Longer battery life

Higher resolution screen

New functions:

    Micrometer gap measurement

    Readings in under 0.5 seconds

Text points provide your audience with a list of phrases that give them context for what you will be speaking about.

Examples of usage:

- sharing a list of rules about room rentals
- sharing a list of tips for creating effective emails

How to create and use this visual

A slide of text points is what many (if not most) bullet point slides should really be. When the points are not hierarchical, you don't need bullet characters and can separate the points with space between the lines. You can still use indents to indicate levels if desired. Create a default layout in PowerPoint that properly aligns each line of text and has extra space between the lines to create the visual separation.

As with bullet points, be cautious about putting too much text on one slide. You slides should not be your speaking notes. Make sure the text will be easy to read when projected. I have done the research on what size font you should use based on the size of the screen and the size of the room. You can see the results at www.PPtFontSizeTable.com. In most situations, you should use a font that is 24 point or larger for text points.

Additional examples

Most accessories are purchased at ABC store with or shortly after device purchase

Device protection accessories bought with device; functionality extensions bought later

Accessory ROI is $13 with Standard accessories more profitable than Smart accessories

Categorization: Entities > Group of items

Text in shapes

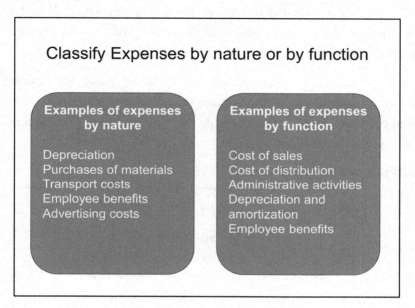

By formatting text in shapes instead of a list of points, it helps the audience see groupings of text and gives a visual break from the typical text slide format.

Examples of usage:

- you have groups of text points that are related to each other
- you have text points that are related, but not hierarchical
- you want to show grouping of certain points

How to create and use this visual

This visual is created by placing shapes on the slide and then adding text to the shape. In PowerPoint, you can format the text within a shape with all the options that text boxes allow: you can set different alignment for different sections of text, you can align the text block at the top or center of the shape, you can set spacing between the lines, you can set text to different colors to provide emphasis, and any other formatting techniques you need. A shape can have one or many lines of text.

Another format is to separate the text boxes with a dashed line. This is a clean look and works well if there are two or three groups of text that you want to display.

When building the shapes on the slide using the animation feature in PowerPoint, you can have shapes appear with all the text or build each text point within the shape one at a time. This gives you more control when explaining the points.

Additional examples

Data Incorporated for Model Develop and Scoring

Internal Data

Line level and account level data

Refreshed monthly

Covered subscription, usage, charge, and derived variables

Diverse data source: Data Warehouse, Billing, Network, Internet, CS (Customer Service)

External Data

Acxiom household demographic information

DnB firmographic data

This example shows two groups of text separated by a light dashed line. Use a muted color for the line so it visually separates the groups of text but is not too prominent.

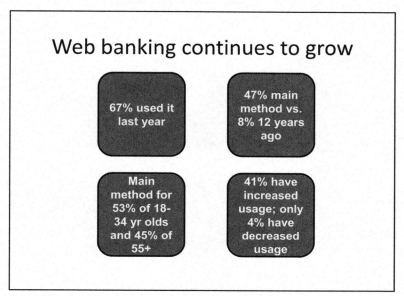

Use colored shapes when it will give a visual change of pace in your presentation, as this example shows.

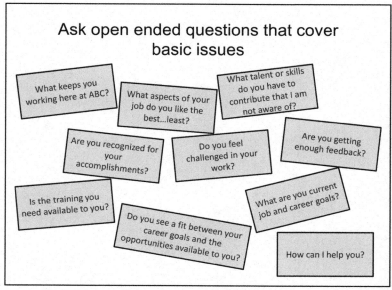

Each of the shapes in this example would be built one at a time so each question can be explained by the presenter.

Category 5: A person, place, or object

The fifth category of visuals is the one that shows a person, place, or object.

I have organized the visuals in this category into the following groups:

- Showing the size of an object
- Little or no explanation required
- Explanation required

On the following pages in this chapter, you will see all of the visuals in this category organized by the groups listed above.

Each group will have an introductory page that has a list of all of the visuals in that group. At the top of the page for each visual you will see how it is categorized under the category, and group. If you need to see a list of all of the visuals in this category, refer to page 21 in the introduction to Step 2.

Category 5: A person, place, or object

Group 1: Showing the size of an object

The first group in this category is messages where you want to show how big an object is.

Here is a list of the visuals in this group:

Group of icons

Categorization: Object > Showing size

Group of icons

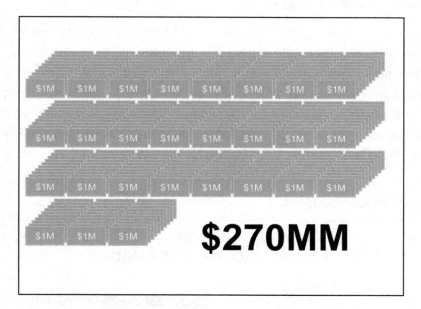

A group of icons shows the audience how large an item is by showing them one icon for each relevant unit used to measure the size of the item.

Examples of usage:

- showing how large the market is for your products
- showing how many steps a customer must go through in order to get a refund
- showing how many steps it takes to set up a vendor in the accounting system

How to create and use this visual

This visual is created by using an icon that represents the unit of measurement for the amount you are showing. This could be dollars (or multiples of dollars such as millions or billions), people, books, cars, steps, or any other unit of measurement. The icon you use can be one you purchased or you can create a simple icon as in the example above. Make sure that you put the correct number of icons on the slide so that the number you are showing is accurately represented by the visual.

To make it easier to create a large number of icons, create the first one and then copy and paste to create more icons. Group a reasonable number, usually a multiple of ten or some easy to understand multiple. Then you can copy and paste the group to create many more icons quickly. If you have a lot to create, as in the example above, group an entire row of icons and copy and paste the row. You can use the Align and Distribute functions to position the icons or groups of icons on the slide.

Additional examples

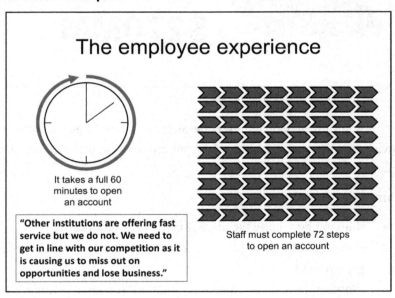

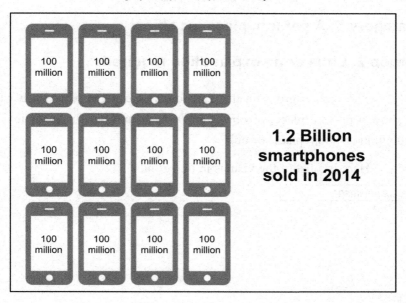

Category 5: A person, place, or object

Group 2: Little or no explanation required

The second group in this category is messages where you want to show a person, place, or object and you do not need a lot of text to explain the person, place, or object.

Here is a list of the visuals in this group:

Full screen image

Categorization: Object > Little explanation required

Full screen image

A full screen image with little or no text makes a strong impact on the audience and, since the image is almost self-explanatory, they understand your message quickly.

Examples of usage:

- you have a photo that is self-explanatory
- you want the photo to set a certain mood with the audience
- the photo will enhance a story you are telling
- you want the photo to make a dramatic impact, but it needs some text to explain the point the photo is making
- you have a high-res photo that you want to use as an opening or closing to your presentation

How to create and use this visual

This visual should make an impact when it is displayed, so you don't want anything distracting from it. After you add the photo to the slide, resize it so it covers the entire slide. You may need to crop it to fit the size of slide you are using. If cropping would remove some key areas of the photo or would result in a low resolution image, place a black rectangle over the entire slide before you add the photo. That way, there is nothing else on the slide except the photo.

If you decide to add a few words on the slide, use a text box on top of the photo. Make the font big enough so it is easy to read. In order to make the text easy to read on the photo, add a contrasting color outline to the text and a Glow to the text in the same color as the outline. Choosing black text with a white outline and glow or white text with a black outline and glow usually work best.

The big issue for many presenters is where to get high resolution images that can be used in a corporate presentation. There are many sources of images to consider:

- Your own photos: if you have taken a great photo, why not use it in your presentation?
- Stock photography sites: there are many stock photo sites where you can purchase photos to use.
- Royalty-free photos: there are many sites that offer photos for use without requiring a payment. This sounds great and it can be, as long as you understand the restrictions on usage. I'll discuss some of these concerns in the next paragraph. In my article at http://paradi.link/Issue313, I list some sites that offer royalty free photos.

Whenever you are using a photo, you need to make sure you have permission to use it in a commercial context. If it is a photo you took, check that it was not taken as part of your employment, as the company will likely then own the rights to the photo. If you have purchased the photo, read the license to make sure you can use it the way you are considering. If you are using a royalty free photo, make sure you understand the license it has been published under. Often photos are published under the Creative Commons license. Be aware that there are different categories of Creative Commons licenses. Many of the popular categories allow you to use the photo only if you agree to release the resulting work into the public domain as well. This means that to use the photo, you have to agree to release your entire presentation, with all the confidential corporate data in it, into the public domain. Not a likely option for most corporate presenters.

I must inform you that I am not a lawyer and nothing I write should be considered as legal advice. You should seek an opinion from a licensed attorney in your jurisdiction to confirm your rights and responsibilities when using images. (I need to say that so I don't get in trouble if someone claims my advice caused them to use an image illegally.)

Why not just do a web search for images and grab one you like? Because if you do, you will likely have violated the copyright of the owner of the image. There are more and more cases of image owners going after those who use an image without purchasing a license. Some of the big stock photography sites have people pursuing this full time. Why take the risk personally or as an organization when there are many legal sources for images?

Additional examples

By using the outline and glow on the text in this example, it is easy to see the text on a background with many colors.

This example shows a picture where no text effects were needed because there was a portion of the picture that provided contrast for the text.

Category 5: A person, place, or object

Group 3: Explanation required

The third group in this category is messages where you want to show a person, place, or object and you need some text to explain the person, place, or object.

Here is a list of the visuals in this group:

Image with callouts
Image with captions

Categorization: Object > Explanation required

Image with callouts

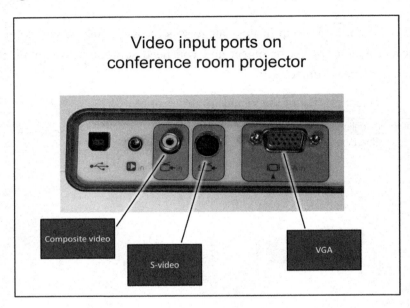

This visual shows an image and uses callouts to indicate important parts of the image to the audience.

Examples of usage:

- showing the key parts of a piece of equipment
- showing a customer where they can get help on your website
- showing someone how to change the settings on their camera's setup screen

How to create and use this visual

Once you have added the image to the slide, you need to make sure that it will effectively communicate your message. Crop the image so you remove any parts that are not important to communicating your message. For example, if you are using a screen capture, crop out the browser toolbar and scrollbars. Once the image is cropped, make it large enough so it is easily seen on the slide. Leave room for the callouts on one or more sides of the image.

The image you use can come from many sources. It could be a photo which can come from any of the sources listed on page 214 in the section on full screen images. It could be a screen capture from a website, smartphone app, or corporate system. It could be an image captured from a PDF document like a table or graph. Or it could be a visual created in illustration or design software. With any of the images you use, make sure they are as high resolution as possible so that they will still look crisp and clear after they have been cropped and resized.

After the image is on the slide, add your callouts. PowerPoint contains a number of good callout shapes you can use. These callouts include a way to point at the important spot of the image and add explanatory text so the audience knows why that spot is important.

There are a few callouts that have boxes and lines. When using these shapes, you may want to add a Glow to the shape (one of the Shape Effects in PowerPoint) in a color that contrasts with the outline color. This makes the line easier to see on backgrounds that do not have a single color (this is demonstrated in the example above with the white glow around the black line).

PowerPoint also includes balloon callout shapes. When using these shapes, set the fill color and outline color to contrasting colors. This makes the point easier to see. Also set the fill color to 10-20% transparency if it covers up part of the image. This will allow the audience to see the image underneath the callout shape.

Additional examples

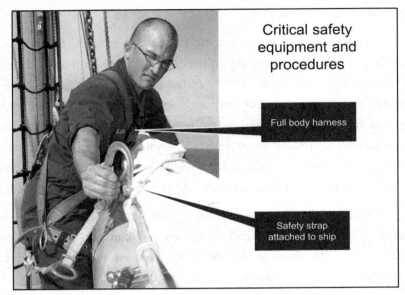

This example uses the rectangle balloon callout shape.

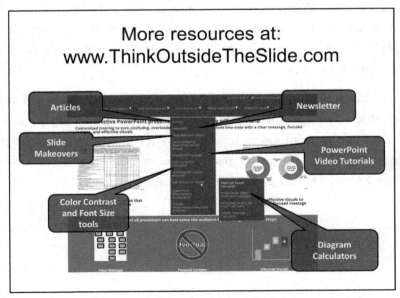

This example uses semi-transparent fills to allow the underlying screen capture to be seen.

Categorization: Object > Explanation required

Image with captions

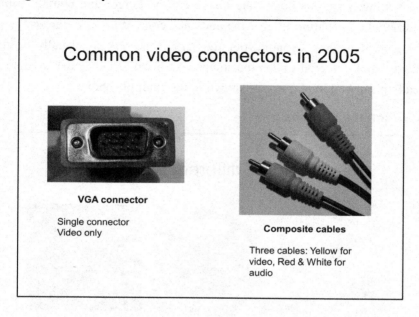

This visual shows an image and uses captions above or below the image to give them context.

Examples of usage:

- showing multiple options for solving a problem
- showing different choices for a purchase
- you want to use an image but also need text to explain the image

How to create and use this visual

Adding the image to the slide for this visual is similar to the image with callouts. Get the appropriate image from one of the sources listed on page 214. Add the image to the slide and crop and resize it. This visual usually includes more than one image, so use the same techniques for each image.

The captions for each image can be above or below the image. Captions above the image are usually short and describe what the image is showing. Captions below the image can be longer and contain some additional explanation to give the audience context for why the image is being used to help explain your message. Captions are usually center aligned and centered under the image. Additional text under a caption heading can be left aligned, as shown in the example above.

Additional examples

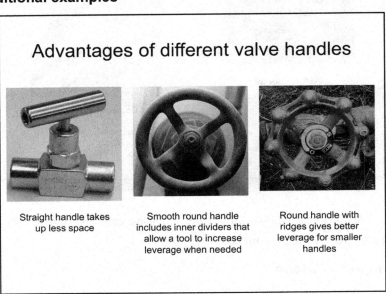

This example shows the captions centered below each image.

Category 6: Example or demonstration

The sixth category of visuals is the one that shows an example or demonstration.

I have organized the visuals in this category into the following groups:

- Written format
- Multimedia format

On the following pages in this chapter, you will see all of the visuals in this category organized by the groups listed above.

Each group will have an introductory page that has a list of all of the visuals in that group. At the top of the page for each visual you will see how it is categorized under the category, and group. If you need to see a list of all of the visuals in this category, refer to page 21 in the introduction to Step 2.

Category 6: Example or demonstration

Group 1: Written format

The first group in this category is messages where the example or demonstration is in written format.

Here is a list of the visuals in this group:

Highlighted text
Quote
Case study

Highlighted text

> # ISAs are required by ABC Corporate Policy 04-103
>
> "All United States and international legal entities involved in the transfer of products, services, property and licensed rights must document this activity in an inter-company contract executed by the legal entities."

This visual shows a passage of text with a highlighted section that indicates to the audience the most important words or phrases in the passage.

Examples of usage:

- highlighting key phrases in a quote from a regulatory document
- emphasizing certain words in a policy

How to create and use this visual

This visual is used when you want to provide proof or show a reason for what you are saying. The text usually comes from an authoritative document such as regulations, policies, procedures, or standards.

Add the text as a text box on the slide, using a font that will be large enough for the audience to easily read the words. Include the source of the text if necessary in a smaller font below the passage. Put the passage in quotes if needed. The text box should not have a fill color because the highlight technique requires a transparent shape to work. If the text is an image taken from another source, such as a PDF document, you will have to make the background of the image transparent. In many cases with this type of image, the Set Transparent Color feature of PowerPoint will allow you to remove the white background of the image.

Once the text is on the slide, you can add the highlight. The highlight is one or more rectangles placed behind the text box in the appropriate spot. There is no highlight text feature in PowerPoint (as there is in Word). For slides that have a white background, a yellow highlight works well because it looks like highlighting on a printed page. Add the highlight shape on top of the text box to get the positioning correct, then move it to a layer behind the text box. To select the highlight shape after it has been moved behind the text box, use the Selection and Visibility pane in PowerPoint.

Additional examples

"The purpose of the Organization is to contribute to peace and security by promoting collaboration among the nations through education, science and culture in order to further universal respect for justice, for the rule of law and for the human rights and fundamental freedoms which are affirmed for the peoples of the world, without distinction of race, sex, language or religion, by the Charter of the United Nations."

UNESCO Charter
(emphasis added)

Just keep the trust and strong relationship I have with my account: Carlos Henderson, Elena May, Daren Cox and Ed Schwartz. They understand my business and I feel we share the same company culture in being dedicated to our customers. My relation with my account team is really a differentiator from others.

ACME Construction, Rudolph Morales, Director of Engineering and Planning

Categorization: Example > Written

Quote

"The only
reason to
give a speech
is to change
the world"

John F. Kennedy

This visual shows a quote and an image of the person who said the quote.

Examples of usage:

- quoting a thought leader in the field to support your point
- quoting a prominent person to show how popular a thought is

How to create and use this visual

This visual is used to add credibility to your message by using the words of a prominent person. While you can use a quote without an image of the person who said it, the image adds to the effectiveness of the visual.

Add the quote to the slide using a text box. The quote is usually in bold, large font, and center or left aligned. The attribution for the quote is placed below the quote in smaller font and right aligned. When using a quote, verify its accuracy with reputable sources. Many common sayings attributed to famous people are actually modified from what the person actually said or the person never actually said what is attributed to them.

When searching for an image of the person, make sure you have permission to use the image. On page 214 in the section on full screen images I discussed copyright issues related to images.

When placing the image and the quote on the slide, the quote is usually placed so the person in the image is looking at the quote. The audience will look where the image is looking, so place the quote where they will naturally look for it.

Additional examples

"The world won't care about your self-esteem. The world will expect you to accomplish something BEFORE you feel good about yourself."

Bill Gates

Categorization: Example > Written

Case study

> # Case study: Consolidation with sustainable solution
>
> **Challenge:**
> Merge several offices into a single site solution
>
> **Cost Impact:**
> All-in lease cost remain the same & meet
> LEED requirements to reduce operating cost
>
> **Solution:**
> 3 Stories of large floor plates allow
> consolidation into a single building with sustainable
> features
>
>
>
> XYZCorporate Office
> Anytown, AK
> 125,000 sq ft; opened Sep '09
>
> **Benefit:**
> Departments easily expand & contract within large open
> floor plates. Project achieved LEED Silver

This visual shows a case study that proves the point you are making.

Examples of usage:

- proving that your solution will solve the problem that a prospect has
- demonstrating that you have the expertise to handle the situation
- proving that your product can withstand the operating conditions

How to create and use this visual

A case study slide should include four sections. First, describe the problem that was faced in the previous situation. Second, what was that problem costing the organization or what opportunity were they missing out on. Third, what solution was provided. And fourth, what was the benefit of that solution. The purpose of a case study is not to brag about past accomplishments, it is to provide evidence of your ability to successfully provide a solution to the problem the audience is facing. Including a photo or testimonial is a good idea to provide further evidence.

Additional examples

Network extender allowed all users in office/warehouse to be connected

Problem & Impact:
Twenty staff can't make calls, receive emails, send texts due to obstructions in 5,000 sq ft mixed use space

Solution:
Use cluster of network extenders to provide strong signal in all areas of the space

Benefit:
All staff can now use cellular services to increase productivity

This example shows how sometimes the problem and impact sections can be combined.

(examples continue on next page)

Case study: Luxury car brand increased visibility with key target market

Challenge: Build interest in latest engineering innovations amongst luxury car enthusiasts

Opportunity: Increase sales

Solution:
- 100% SOV tablet app featuring content from premiere publisher, CarEnthusiasts.com
- App updated daily with new original features, articles, imagery & videos
- Integrated brand placement throughout the app

Result: 12,000 app downloads and 34,500 click-throughs from app ads

When each section has a lot of text, as in this example, it is even more important to make the headings stand out with bold or larger text.

Category 6: Example or demonstration

Group 2: Multimedia format

The second group in this category is messages where the example or demonstration is in multimedia format.

Here is a list of the visuals in this group:

Audio clip
Video clip

Audio clip

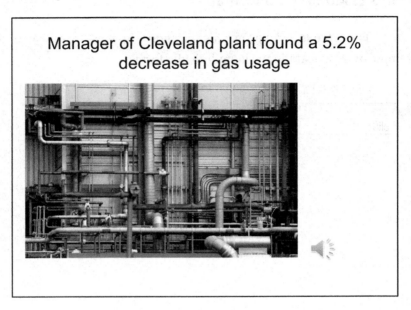

This visual includes an audio file that is played for the audience. The audio is of someone backing up or supporting the point you are making

Examples of usage:

- when you want the audience to hear a quote as it was spoken at the time
- when you are demonstrating what it would sound like over a phone, as in an example customer service call

How to create and use this visual

PowerPoint allows you to add an audio clip from a file. The clip should be clear, last no more than 30-45 seconds, and be relevant to the point you are making. Prepare the clip in audio editing software so it is loud enough to hear easily and contains only the portion of the recording most relevant to the message. If the clip is unclear, consider adding a transcript of the audio so the audience understands what was said. With the proliferation of video today, audio clips should only be used when a video is not available. If possible, include a photo of the person who is speaking or a photo of the object they are speaking about so that the audience has a visual to go along with the audio they hear.

When introducing the audio clip before you play it, make sure you give the audience the context: let them know who is speaking, what they are speaking about, in what context the recording was done if that is relevant, why you feel this clip is relevant to the point you are making, and any particular spots in the audio you want them to pay attention to. With a proper introduction, the audience can focus on what is said and will understand how it supports your message.

Additional examples

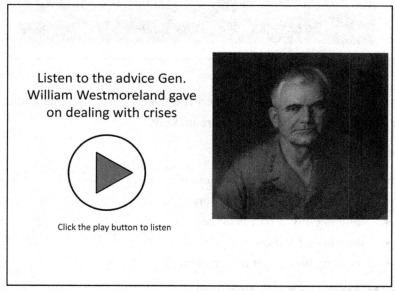

Listen to the advice Gen. William Westmoreland gave on dealing with crises

Click the play button to listen

If the slide will be presented by someone else or it will be e-mailed to others, you may need to include an instruction to play the audio clip, as shown in this example.

Categorization: Example > Multimedia

Video clip

Proposed location is ideal for OTM's distribution center

This visual includes a video file that is played for the audience. The video supports the point you are making.

Examples of usage:

- showing a customer testimonial
- showing how a machine works
- showing how a part is made
- showing a location
- showing how to set up a system

How to create and use this visual

Like audio files described on page 234, PowerPoint allows you to insert a video file on a slide. And similar to the audio file, the video needs to first be prepared in a video editing program to make sure it is high quality, only contains the relevant segments, and is loud enough that the audio can be clearly heard. The preference is to insert the video on the slide instead of playing the video in a media player program or playing it from the Web in a browser. Both of these methods interrupt the flow of your presentation.

Once the video clip is inserted on the slide, make it as large as possible so it is easy to see. If you want only the video on the slide and it does not fill the slide, place a black rectangle underneath the video that covers the entire slide. Set the animation timing of the video so it plays on an animation advance or as soon as the slide is displayed. This gives you time to properly introduce the video before it is played.

Like an audio clip, the video should be properly introduced so the audience has the context for the video. See the suggestions in the audio clip section on page 235 for what to include in the introduction of the video before it is played.

Additional examples

Step 3: Focus the audience during delivery

When you are delivering your presentation, you want the audience to be focused on the point you are making and the visual that illustrates your point. Sometimes you need to direct them to a specific spot on the visual or explain the visual one step at a time so they follow your explanation.

Too often presenters resort to using a laser pointer to try to focus the audience. A laser pointer often does not work well because it can be hard to see, too small to follow if the presenter is moving it, and it forces the presenter to face the screen instead of the audience.

There are three techniques you should consider that will help focus the audience while you are presenting:

1. Callouts
2. Builds
3. Organizing information

Callouts

A callout allows you to focus the audience on the most important area of the visual. On page 219 I discussed adding callouts to an image. Both types of callouts discussed on that page can be useful for any type of visual. The box and line callouts allow you to point to a specific spot on the visual and add explanatory text so the audience knows why it is important. The balloon callout shapes are slightly larger, but still allow you to direct the audience's attention while including explanatory text.

Presenters often use a simple shape, such as a circle or rectangle, to indicate important areas on a visual. This is simulating what they would do with a pen if they were drawing on a printed page. I don't think using a shape alone is enough. You also need the explanatory text so the audience knows why you want them to focus on that spot. Add that text in a text box close to the shape or use one of the box and line callouts to place the explanatory text farther away from the shape. The text should be short, usually just a few words. It should be able to be read in one to two seconds so the audience can return their focus to your explanation of why this spot is important to them.

Builds

In many of the visuals throughout this book, I have suggested that building the visual one element at a time would make it more effective when it is presented. The reason builds are important in delivery is because it allows you to give the audience context before they come to a conclusion. If you display all parts of the visual at once, two things happen.

First, the audience does not listen to your explanation because they immediately look at the visual and start interpreting it. Research cited in John Medina's book "Brain Rules" tells us we can't read and listen at the same time. Second, they draw a conclusion about the visual before you have had a chance to give your explanation. The conclusion they come to may be different from the one you wanted them to come to, and it will be difficult to get them to change their mind.

To build your visual piece by piece, the best approach is to use the Animation feature of PowerPoint. This allows you to control when each element appears on the slide. Stick to the simple effects, such as the Appear, Fade, or Wipe effects. Don't use the swirling, twirling, bouncing effects that make your presentation appear unprofessional.

Test the speed of any Wipe animations to make sure they happen slow enough that the audience will be able to see the motion of the slide element. I use the Wipe effect when drawing a line from left to right on a line graph or when growing columns on a column graph from the axis up.

Organizing information

If you have a complex idea to present, you need to organize it so the audience can easily follow your explanation.

If you have a complex visual, such as a large screen capture or a complex wiring diagram, it will be overwhelming to try to present it all as one visual. Organize your explanation and visuals to make it easier for the audience. Show them the whole visual to give them context. Use a shape, usually a rectangle, to indicate the one section of the visual you want to discuss in detail. Then show a visual of just the small area you want to discuss. Use callouts or builds as needed with just that one area.

If you have a long list of related points to discuss, such as the sales trend in each of 15 product lines, don't show all 15 lines on one graph. Organize the products into natural groups, such as hardware, software, and services. Start with a graph that shows the trends in each of the three groups. This allows you to discuss trends at a higher level. Then you can use a graph that shows the trends of the specific products in one or more groups to further explain the overall trends. Whether it is a list of product sales trends or a list of features of the new accounting system, organize the list into natural groups, explain the groups, and then go into detail on one or more of the groups as needed.

Excluded visuals

In the previous sections of this book, you may have noticed that certain visuals, such as stacked column graphs, pie charts with different colored wedges, or Venn diagrams are missing. Why did I exclude them? Because I think there are better options, and/or because they are too complex or academic to be used in typical business presentations.

In the next few pages I will share the visuals I excluded, why I left them out, and what alternatives from the previous sections could be used instead (if applicable).

Multi-colored pie chart

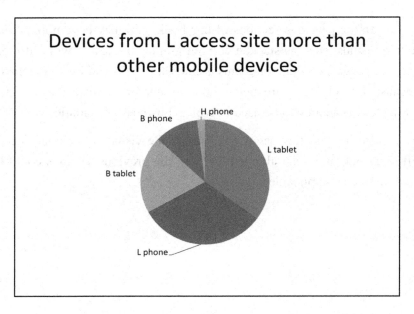

Why it was excluded

The typical use of a multi-colored pie chart is to show a comparison of the sizes of each wedge. In the above example, the audience is supposed to compare the wedges to determine which devices are most common and by how much. This is very difficult to do with a pie chart because it is difficult to tell the difference between sizes of wedges, especially if the values are close to each other. For example, in the example above, is the red wedge larger or smaller than the blue wedge? It is smaller, but it is difficult to determine. That is why a multi-colored pie chart was not included in the list of visuals for the message of comparing values to each other in a single data series.

Alternative visuals to use instead

The best alternative to a multi-colored pie chart is a bar chart (page 50) because you can easily see which bar is longer.

Stacked column or bar graphs

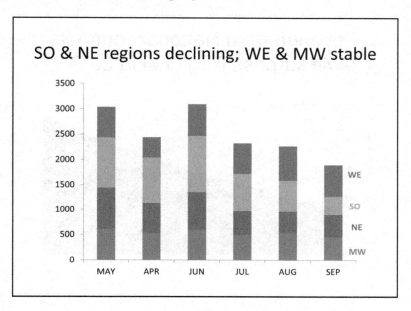

Why it was excluded

A stacked column or bar graph is difficult for the audience to understand because it contains multiple messages. Determine which message you are communicating and select an alternative visual that communicates just that one message. If you have multiple messages you want to communicate, create multiple slides and select an appropriate visual for each message.

Alternative visuals to use instead

If your message is comparing the heights of the total columns, use a column graph instead (page 46). If your message is comparing how one segment compares to the whole in the different time periods, use a multiple 100% stacked bar chart or column graph (pages 99 and 102). If your message is to show the change in each segment across the time periods, use a multiple line graph (page 125).

Stacked area graph

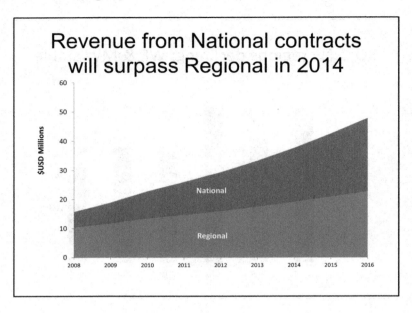

Why it was excluded

A stacked area graph, similar to the stacked column or bar graphs on page 245, is difficult for the audience to understand because it contains multiple messages. Determine which message you are communicating and select an alternative visual that communicates just that one message. If you have multiple messages you want to communicate, create multiple slides and select an appropriate visual for each message.

Alternative visuals to use instead

If your message is showing the overall trend, use a single line graph instead (page 119). If your message is comparing how one segment compares to the whole in the different time periods, use a 100% stacked bar chart or column graph (pages 99 and 102). If your message is to show the change in each segment across the time periods, use a multiple line graph (page 125).

Venn diagram

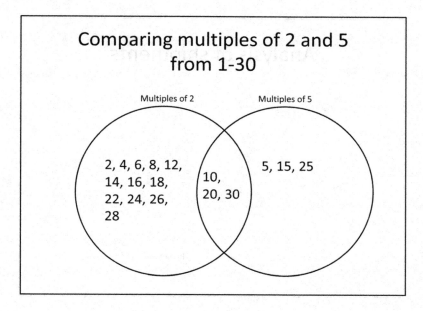

Why it was excluded

A Venn diagram comes from set theory in mathematics. It is used primarily in science and education and I have rarely ever seen an appropriate use in a business setting.

Data scientist visuals

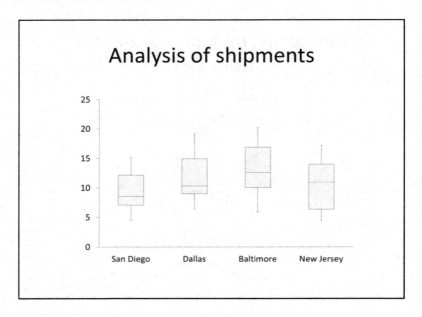

Why they were excluded

Visuals that come from the world of data science or data visualization such as boxplots, x-y plots, scatter diagrams, histograms, bubble charts, Marimekko charts, Sankey diagrams, and others are used for specific science usage, not for business purposes. You may use some of these visuals during your analysis of data, but the visual is too complex for a business audience. Select the key message you want to communicate and choose a visual that communicates that one message.

Alternative visuals to use instead

The alternatives will vary based on the message, but as an example, here are some visuals that would work for different messages that could be important in a boxplot such as the example above. If the message is comparing the median values to each other, use a column graph of the median values (page 46). If the message is comparing the ranges of values in the second and third quartile (the box in the boxplot), use a column graph of the ranges (page 65). If the message is comparing the size of one quartile compared to the total range, use a 100% stacked bar chart (page 93). If the message is comparing the trend of the median over time, use a single line graph (page 119).

A histogram is just a column graph that compares values organized a particular way, so use the advice on page 46 when creating and using column graphs to create a histogram.

Bubble charts contain multiple messages, so split the individual messages into separate slides. The main message is usually comparing the size of the bubbles to each other, which is a message about comparing values to each other in a single data series (page 46-62). You can use proportional shapes if you want a similar look (page 53).

A Marimekko chart compares values to each other in a single data series and uses proportional shapes arranged into a larger shape. You can use a treemap (page 96) or proportional shapes (page 53) instead.

A Sankey diagram shows a total value being broken down into segments and sub-segments. This type of message can be communicated using a stacked bar breakdown chart instead (page 112).

Slopegraph

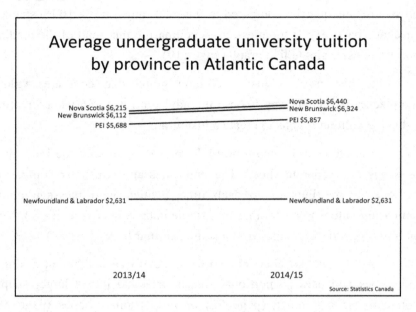

Why it was excluded

Slopegraphs were created by Edward Tufte and are popular with data scientists. They are primarily used to show the comparison of the slopes between two or more values. It is difficult for a business audience to accurately compare the slope of two or more lines and easily draw a conclusion. Proponents of slopegraphs suggest that they can communicate messages of rank, value, and change in value in one visual. This does not fit with my approach of one message per slide, which I have found works better for business presentations.

Alternative visuals to use instead

If the slope of the line is the important message, then I suggest that the difference between the two values, either absolute or relative, is the key measure and can be shown using a column graph (page 46) or bar chart (page 50). If there is a second message about ranking or comparison of values, use a second visual on a second slide.

Radar chart

Why it was excluded

Radar charts (and a closely related visual called a Nightingale Rose chart) compare values to each other using a scale that radiates out from the center of a circular shape. It is very difficult to compare values when the scale for each value is in a different place. The resulting shape does not have significance other than it connects the values. When you add a second data series, it becomes even more confusing.

Alternative visuals to use instead

Instead of such a complicated visual, use a column graph (page 46) or bar chart (page 50) for a single data series. For two data series, use a multiple width overlapping column graph (page 67). For three or more data series, use a small multiples visual (page 81).

SmartArt

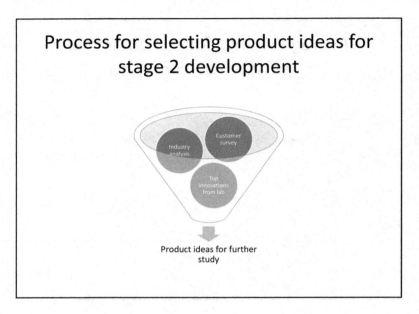

Why it was excluded

SmartArt was created by Microsoft in an attempt to make it easy for presenters to use visuals instead of bullet points. The issue is that, like many lists of visuals, it is organized by type of diagram, not by what message you are communicating. When most presenters are selecting SmartArt, they just scroll through the examples and find one they like based on how it looks. Rarely do they look at what message it is communicating.

PowerPoint does tell you what message the SmartArt diagram should be used for, but most presenters never look at the description. For example, the description for the funnel diagram shown above starts with, "Use to show the filtering of information or how parts merge into a whole. Emphasizes the final outcome."

Some SmartArt diagrams can be used to create visuals described in the previous sections, but most are just design oriented visuals that can be replaced by simpler visuals.

Alternative visuals to use instead

Use simple visuals instead of the fancy ones in SmartArt. For the funnel visual above, if the message is how the number of options is reduced along the way, use proportional shapes (page 53) to show the reduction in options at each stage. If the message is about the process used to filter options, use a process diagram (page 135-145). If the message is about how different inputs add to a conclusion, use an equation diagram (page 193). There is almost always a simpler way to show the message instead of using a SmartArt diagram.

Additional Resources

One of the problems with publishing a book is that I find new content I want to include right after it is published. Or I have examples that can't be used in the book without going through an onerous permission process. Or there are videos or detailed tutorials that don't really fit the format or style of the book. As an author, I struggle with what to do about this.

I want you to always be able to access any new ideas I come up with on selecting and creating effective visuals. I want you to see additional examples from media or other sources. I want to provide you with tutorials that walk you through how to create these visuals in Excel or PowerPoint.

So I have created a special page on my website that will contain all of this and hopefully more. It already contains content that I found or created in the past, and content I created during the writing of this book. More will be added as time goes on.

To access this special page, go to the website for this book, www.SelectEffectiveVisuals.com. Click on the link you see there for owners of this book. Enter the password SEV62 (all letters are capitals) when prompted. You will then see a list of additional resources and links, organized in the same order as the book.

If you find a resource that should be included on this web page, email me at Dave@ThinkOutsideTheSlide.com and I will check it out.

Alphabetical index of visuals

Customized Training Workshops

When you bring me in to conduct a customized workshop, it will be different than other presentation training. I don't teach presentation skills like how to stand, gesture, or breathe. I don't teach "every feature" basic PowerPoint courses. I teach business professionals how to create a PowerPoint presentation that has a clear message, focused content, and effective visuals.

Your staff are learning from a true expert. I am one of fourteen people in North America to be currently recognized by Microsoft with the PowerPoint Most Valuable Professional Award for my contributions to the PowerPoint presentation community. I have a degree in Chemical Engineering, and an MBA, so I can understand the details of your presentations and the communication challenges of business professionals.

Every workshop is customized to the type of content your team presents. This is not a standard course that is the same regardless of your individual needs. Customized slide makeovers are integral to every workshop. I collect samples from the participants in advance and prepare makeovers so they can see how the ideas apply to the types of information they have to present. This is always the highlight of the workshop.

Participants receive a detailed handout, all the slide makeovers in PowerPoint format, and a customized email of links to articles and videos for further reference. Participants walk out with a new expectation of what an effective PowerPoint presentation looks like and many practical ideas they can apply immediately to improve their presentations. My clients tell me that no one does what I do.

Call me at (905) 510-4911 (Eastern time zone) or e-mail me at Dave@ThinkOutsideTheSlide.com to discuss how I can customize a workshop for your group.

CPSIA information can be obtained
at www.ICGtesting.com
Printed in the USA
FSOW04n1351240816
23922FS